MEMENTOS, ARTIFACTS, AND HALLUCINATIONS

from the Ethnographer's Tent

MEMENTOS, ARTIFACTS, AND HALLUCINATIONS

from the Ethnographer's Tent

EDITED BY
RON EMOFF AND DAVID HENDERSON

Routledge
Taylor & Francis Group

NEW YORK AND LONDON

Published in 2002 by
Routledge
29 West 35th Street
New York, New York 10001
www.routledge-ny.com

Published in Great Britain by
Routledge
11 New Fetter Lane
London EC4P 4EE
www.routledge.co.uk

Routledge is an imprint of the Taylor & Francis Group.

10 9 8 7 6 5 4 3 2 1

Library of Congress Cataloging-in-Publication Data

Mementos, artifacts, and hallucinations from the ethnographer's tent / edited by
Ron Emoff and David Henderson.
   p. cm.
  Includes bibliographical references.
  ISBN 0-415-93545-8 (acid-free paper)—ISBN 0-415-93546-6 (pbk. : acid-free paper)
    1. Ethnology—Field work. 2. Ethnologists—Biography. I. Emoff, Ron. II. Henderson, David, 1968–

  GN346 .M46 2002
  305.8'007'23—dc21

2002021967

Contents

Introduction

RON EMOFF AND DAVID HENDERSON

> Wouldn't you say any attempt to tell a story is an attempt to tell the truth? It's the technique you use in the telling that is either more or less plausible. Sometimes the most direct way to tell the truth is to tell a totally implausible story, like a myth. That way you avoid the muddle of pretending the story ever happened, or will happen.
> —Ursula K. Le Guin, "Coming Back from the Silence"

When we write about our lives and the people who inhabit them, we often find ourselves searching for words that depict our experiences clearly and provocatively. In writing ethnography, though, a common ploy is to move our experiences to the background while placing in the foreground what we have come to know about the experiences, perceptions, and lives of the people with whom we have lived. Franz Boas, one of the ancestral spirits of American anthropology today, lived among and wrote about the Kwakiutl of the northwest coast of North America in the late 1800s and early 1900s. While he collected an immense amount of information from one particular Kwakiutl man, George Hunt, there is very little in Boas's work about George Hunt himself.[1] We read instead about Kwakiutl social organization, religious practices, grammatical forms, and expressive culture. This, as James Clifford, Dick Cushman, George Marcus, and others have made clear, has been the basic narrative formula of ethnography—turning individuals, isolated moments of talk, and relatively brief encounters into coherent depictions of a people and their way of life.[2]

Sometimes, strange tales emerge when we condense, streamline, and translate the desiderata of our fieldwork. Margaret Mead, for example, has been criticized for making essentializing and inaccurate comments about a particular group of people in Papua New Guinea, using information given to her by a neighboring group. One of these groups lived by fishing, and the other practiced agriculture; each group told myths about their superiority over the other. But Mead, with her limited knowledge of Papuan speech genres, did not recognize what she heard as caricature and confabulation. Rather, she apparently felt compelled to author an ethnographic "truth" about one group of Papuans, based upon the comments of the other group.[3]

Certainly, ethnographers have toiled assiduously to learn how to ascertain whether or not the information that they report is accurate. Many also have recognized that accuracy is not always ensured and enshrined within the collected data. Most importantly, some have argued that the conventional narrative strategies of ethnography leave little room to say anything about the research process itself. Turning *the* Nuer or *the* Newars into narratives about social structure and cultural patterns, for example, often omits much of the experience of doing ethnography and bypasses much of the reality of being there. This is not to say that understanding and representing something of the whole of culture has not remained of utmost importance in the work of anthropologists, ethnomusicologists, folklorists, and others; it has. But are there ways we might also explore a third space of research—a space that encompasses how others inscribe structures and patterns upon us, how we write these upon others, and how we brood over these transformations in the course of writing.

When we frame ethnographic narratives as realistic depictions of what happens among other peoples in other lands, or as overarching explications of how society or culture is constituted, we sometimes manage to slip around any troublesome differences of opinion as to what happened. We slide into a space where modes of representation operate separately from modes of production, where writing ethnography erases some of the muddle of doing ethnography. While we could take ethnography to be a matter of explaining and accounting for what happened, we also might undertake it as an exploration of the ways by which knowledge and culture come into being. Ethnography is clearly not just the work of the ethnographer. When ethnographers are at work, the people with whom they have lived are at work as well, struggling with the complexities of making meaning through discourse and making sense through observation. One way to do ethnography is to explore the unfolding of ethnographic events in ways that shake the author's faith in fixed interpretations, ways that reiterate that the meanings of events are never secure, ways that clarify that these meanings are socially produced and historically situated. Writing then becomes, in part, less the mastery of a form of knowledge and more a collection of excerpts, outtakes from a continuous conversation about what happens on the edges of multiple forms of knowledge.

Rethinking ethnography as open-ended rather than finished, then, some ethnographers have explored other narrative strategies for representing what they come to know, other ways of writing people. Their goals have been to tell something else of what is out there, huge and unwieldy as "out there" is; to explore other threads in the social fabric of a place, a fabric that is rent with irreconcilable differences of opinion and points of view; and to explore the possibilities of engaging the distinctive unfolding of life in other places and times.

Edmund Carpenter, a Canadian anthropologist who traveled and researched widely and briefly became an American media icon, once compiled a collection of fieldnotes in which he had made brief observations about the response of peoples everywhere to the electronic media that were becoming pervasive tools for creating, representing, and imagining just about anything. These were included in his book, *Oh, What a Blow That Phantom Gave*

Me! (1974). In it, he confessed that "in glancing through these notes recently, I found the observations superficial, the comments petty" (71). But he recognized their value in addressing moments in fieldwork that were often elided in ethnographic writing, and he "decided to include a number of them here because they refer to events which anthropologists rarely acknowledge" (71). In this volume, we have brought together writers who try to depict such events and who admit their own struggles with representing them. They acknowledge events that might have been left buried in their notes or memories and try to overcome their inclinations to write about particular things in particular ways.

Culture, the presumed ground of our writing, has been depicted as many things—as predicament, as locale or vehicle of critique, as site of being-at-home-in-the-world, and, of course as something good to write about.[4] While perhaps living up to any or all of these things, culture comes into our imaginations and intellects through procedures of recounting, often laden with significant interruptions in time, place, and perception. Such spans of experience create varying modes of tension, often implicit, between the specific cultural field and writers and readers of culture themselves. As we read them, though, ethnographic monographs are more than mere representations of different practices, peoples, and places. We are privileged, sometimes again more implicitly than candidly, to be given not simply a representation of culture itself, but a view or sense of a complex system of interactions through which a cultural entity comes to (literary) life and through which it can be taken as truth.

In this book, we are concerned less with unveiling and categorically asserting cultural truths *for* other people and more with passing on varied ways of experiencing distant places—whether such places exist out there in the world or right here at home. The authors for the most part make no pretense about the role of self as mediating body through which meaning must in these cases pass. Yet these offerings are not meant as self-indulgent exercises in reflexivity. They tell of a confluence of individual reflection—of thought processes, critique, and imaginative extrapolation—

with shared, or at least collective, experience in the field. Such a confluence here extends (writing about) culture into realms of creativity, feeling, humor, and reflection often omitted from scholarly writings. The "mementos, artifacts, and hallucinations" of our title are outtakes—the cutting room floor is analogous to their frequently neglected position in a scholarly milieu that often takes "ethnography" to be a realm composed exclusively of information and knowledge. It is not our intention to create a dichotomous relation between a "real" world out there and a ground created through the expressive liberties we have taken here. In other words, we do not for the most part think here in terms of creating representations that transmit merely an interfered-with aura of essential realities in the world. Rather, of importance in this volume is the aura itself that is created when we step onto foreign ground to engage—indeed to become immersed in—others' lives. These chapters explore the production of truth through the acts of writing and reading, and work to create the sense of being there that underlies or even provides an often unstated foundation for the experiences that allow the writing of culture. These chapters address rather than evade the question, "How do you *know*?"

We approach delicately the matter of introducing these assembled outtakes, for each one speaks eloquently for itself. A few words about how each contributes to the spirit of the whole, however, help explain the assemblage. The order in which the chapters appear creates a counterpoint of styles and issues. Kirin Narayan's voice sounds quite different from Karen Tranberg Hansen's, and Amitava Kumar's accent sounds nothing like Ben Feinberg's. Yet the montage of styles, like any intentional juxtaposing of materials, invites readers to absorb thematic similarities along and across the borders between chapters. Several authors—especially Katherine Hagedorn, Karen Tranberg Hansen, and Laurel Kendall—address the issues involved in their ethnographic work more directly. When these issues emerge momentarily, it becomes evident that the narrative styles in all of the chapters have been working to raise and discuss the same issues.

Andrew Causey, engulfed in the sounds and scents of Sumatra, writes of his own loneliness, of his claustrophobia during the rainy season, and of his wavering uncertainty about the existence of spirits in his surroundings in "Samosir's Dark Rains." Although his carving teacher's family is Christian, they also tell stories of *begu,* or ghosts. Causey's grappling with local actualities of spirits is counterpoised by the apparent ease with which local people assimilate and incorporate sometimes disparate belief systems. Having lived in Austin while doing his doctoral work at the University of Texas, Andrew must regularly remind himself, "This is not Texas." Just as monsoon mold creeps through his home in Sumatra, so, too, do Toba Batak belief systems begin to seep through him, and the chapter vividly demonstrates the effect of place—seen and unseen, heard and unheard—on the construction and elaboration of the ethnographer's realities.

Katherine Hagedorn moves deftly back and forth between critical and descriptive languages in "Sacred Secrets: Lessons with Francisco." She tells of her drumming lessons with a Santería drummer who makes use of constant linguistic code switching in his communications with her. Does he do this to confound Hagedorn, or to maintain an ethnographic upper hand? She suggests that rather than working to gain some mode of ascendancy in the immediate moment, Francisco instead creates a "personal creole" with which he "speaks in the margins." He shifts persistently in language use between the sacred/secret realm of the initiated and Katherine's world, the world of the noninitiate, revealing just enough of the secretive without giving up the sacred/secret itself. Occasionally, Hagedorn steps back from her lessons and raises questions about the processes through which ethnographers acquire knowledge of ritual and ritual performance. In her focus on language, she provides a subtle yet playful exploration of the collaborative nature of translation throughout this chapter.

Ron Emoff, in "Wildness in the Heart of Town," writes of how in Madagascar many people speak with a mixture of fear, reverence, and disgust about Antandroy, a Malagasy group from the southern part of the island. Members of this mythologized group often leave their own regional homeland to search for wage labor in a distant east-coast port town, a place where they are often shunned. Elucidating a sense of how different Malagasy groups create social and geographical distance through their constructions of place and identity, Emoff also conveys his sense of discomfort with the numerous imbalances of working and living among a distant group of people, particularly these Malagasy people for whom he has an intense fondness. He describes a dual positioning of himself as subject of and within "the field."

In "Ethnography and Fiction: Where is the Border?" Kirin Narayan points out the dangers involved in delving too far into fictional accounts, reminding us that anthropology's value lies in "the importance of close, respectful attention to the lives of other *actual* people that characterizes fieldwork" (1999, 143). Her contribution to this volume shows beautifully how fictional narrative styles sometimes help us carve detailed descriptions out of ethnographic experience. And while she focuses in "The God of Doorways" on the congenial and densely layered mix of voices surrounding the ethnographer, she also raises questions of how the ethnographer's past infiltrates and shapes not only perceptions of the present, but also the events of the present.

Underlying Karen Tranberg Hansen's "A Touch of Danger" is the sense of apprehension and fear that overtakes her when an imposing and powerful male military figure in Zambia interferes with her research. This encounter brings the politics of ethnography into sharp focus, and the ensuing events shuffle and rearrange the relations between ethnographers, subjects, and their presumed readers. As George Marcus notes in *Ethnography through Thick and Thin,* "the future of critical ethnography itself depends on an understanding of its relationships and affinities to critical sensibilities within other power/knowledges" (1998, 206), and Hansen's work describes this sort of understanding in its making. As Emoff does in his chapter, she expresses this in terms of the desires of ethnographic "subjects" to write themselves or to influence what will be written about them.

As in much scholarship, this volume bespeaks an inherent inequity—the majority of contributors are from the United States, and the ethnographic sites they have chosen are not. An exception is Amitava Kumar, who writes, in "Leaving My Father's House," of his experiences of coming to, living, and working in the United States. Here America is the "other place," the foreign land out there. Remarkable in this chapter is the intensity of India's presence; this is not so much an ethnography of America as an ethnography of an Indian's existence in America. Through writing, the place Kumar inhabits fades and the place that he has been takes on the character of the real, seeping around every corner of everyday life in the United States. Indeed, each of the chapters in this volume conveys some sense of dis-ease with being in varied, distant places—each of us has to some degree been recentered through the experience of being in varied ways "out there."

Rather than move back and forth between different narrative registers, as several authors in this volume do, Ben Feinberg works to blur the separate voices in his writing. "Miguel Alemán and His Dam" compels us to dwell momentarily within its narrative, not letting us hear people from a distance and not allowing us to step back and examine the events that unfold. Feinberg never tells us who narrates his chapter, and his characters do not tell us much about the narrator—an unusual tactic in ethnography as well as in fiction. At the end of his book *The Location of Culture,* Homi Bhabha reminds us that "we must not merely change the *narratives* of our histories, but transform our sense of what it means to live, to be, in other times and different spaces, both human and historical" (1994, 256). This is precisely what Feinberg does here, using writing to transform our sense of what it means to live, to be in rural Mexico (as husband, as father, and as godfather, rather than simply as native).

Laurel Kendall, in "The Battered Wife's Tale," makes us listen to something that even she did not necessarily want to hear and forces us to question the relation between the narrative strategies that people use with us and the narrative strategies that we use to let them have their say. As Kendall talks us through an interview of a young woman in Seoul, she shows that goals and desires emerge from the narrative act itself and that narratives are not just utterances that follow from preconceived notions but are performances that continuously interact with and reflect back upon everchanging notions. This makes her work a critical contribution, a centerpiece that displays how the concerns of this volume are embedded simultaneously in doing and writing ethnography.

In excavating tales from our ethnographic work, we are always wary of having our experiences collapse in upon us. As Kirin Narayan points out, in the essay cited above (1999, 143–144), "if one is free to invent other people and their lives, why even bother with the inconvenient dislocations and anguished ethical ambiguities of fieldwork?" Such inventions would locate us in a very different world, a world built around the author, a world made up of flat surfaces reflecting always inward. The first pages of David Henderson's "The Freak Street Riots of '59" drop us into a world that seems to be entirely of his own making—after all, the narrator begins talking some years after the publication of the account and tells a story of something that happened in 2002. Yet it is clear that he is not "free to invent other people," but indeed constrains his inventions by locating his characters in the midst of the "anguished ethical ambiguities of fieldwork," and he uses his anachronistic parody of Nepali political satires to focus upon very real Nepali concerns regarding cultural commodification and globalization.

We close this volume with Ruth Behar's "The Last Time Tere Danced a Rumba," which, like Kirin Narayan's work, skillfully weaves together ethnography, autobiography, and fiction. Her narrative makes heartbreakingly clear how "the outsider self never simply stands outside" (Abu-Lughod 1991, 141) and how outsider selves are often at the same time insider selves "offering their own, more complex and more lacerating representations" (Behar 1996, 162). Examining the relations between place and identity among Jews in Cuba, she vividly recapitulates the themes of this book. How can we more effectively represent the places we have inhabited and worked in? How can we use narrative styles to situate the people who have taught us what we know about those places? How can we clarify the work these people have done on us without placing ourselves in the foreground of our narratives?

Several common practices and strategies become apparent from reading the work as a whole: these include the twin practices of erasure and disclosure, the confluences and divergences of place and identity, and the mimesis of others' inscriptive or performative genres within our ethnographies.

Some authors have deliberately erased themselves from their narratives, effectively writing themselves out of the picture. One convention of ethnographic writing indeed has been the writing out of the author, in an attempt to compile and convey an objectivity, an informational certainty. Here the authors that remove themselves in part from their narratives do so to trade places, to put themselves into the experiential space of others, and in turn to allow others to speak more immediately through them and their tales. This is a reciprocal form of possession, one in which the body of the ethnographer is inhabited by the voice of the other, while the ethnographer inhabits the other temporarily. On one hand, the disjunction between author and narrator—whether the writer appears as one of the characters in the narrative or assumes the shape of a narrator masked or transformed—in part makes it easier to critique one's own ethnographic practice. On the other hand, the writing of self as other opens up the performative dimensions of cultural and social knowledge.

A related move in some of these chapters is the emergence of a need among ethnographic "subjects" to write themselves, a desire to disclose poignant fragments of their lives, a compulsion to influence what is written about them. In doing ethnography, we find ourselves grappling—ethically, sentimentally, intellectually, spiritually—with the numerous imbalances of working and living among a distant group of people. Sometimes we choose to hear these imbalances as noise—noise that is inevitably silenced in the writing and editing of the multitude of voices that resound throughout our research. Yet it is clear that some of these voices have continued to haunt us. Having asked to be let into others' worlds, we have expected to mediate some of the pains, struggles, and hardships associated with those worlds. Rarely, though, did we anticipate how powerfully the stories and lives of others would resonate within us, even from afar. Later, situating ourselves some distance from our collected and recollected fieldwork, we found ourselves surrounded by the words and worlds we left behind. Through the amassed memory of their telling, the stories others have told us demanded to be written. By giving voice to these stories, we assert the collaborative nature of fieldwork once again, showing how our work is never fully ours.

A third strategy in many of the following chapters is the creation of dissonance between place and identity. Places shift underneath our feet, both in doing and in writing ethnography. For ethnographers, fieldwork is a deliberate displacement of identity, an immersion in others' identities, and we are incapable at any given outset of predicting the ramifications of the venture, either for ourselves or for those with whom we have chosen to work. The fluidity of relations between place and identity, however, acts in counterpoint with ongoing efforts to fix those relations. We call upon others to speak for themselves and their places and are called upon to speak for our own places, in relatively fixed terms. Yet even in fieldwork, our explications of peoples and places, all collected diligently from a variety of sources, appear immediately suspect. We quickly recognize how our narratives are contingent upon a particular way of understanding how people are indexical of places at the same time that places are indexical of people. It is possible to disrupt these interpretive inclinations, however, by focusing on the moments in which the familiarity of place and identity dissolve. This volume, in particular, highlights the sense of displacement through which identities move into and out of focus.

All of the chapters in this volume avow that style and form matter just as much as content and that experimenting with form offers opportunities to convey information and experience provocatively. Several authors, however, explore the relations between the spoken and written genres that they research and the written genres that they produce, making use in print of the narrative styles and forms through which their ethnographic worlds have been collaboratively built. Especially for those of us who focus on expressive culture, it is imperative to convey in writing something of the experience of the genres we research. Ethnomusicology and folklore in particular are disciplines in which the transcription of some part of a performance has long been important, yet the incapacity of written forms to convey the experience of participation has remained troublesome. This is due in part to the fact that doing so effectively or even adequately appears to move us out of the realm of scholarship and into the realm of performance. Infusing our writing with the poetic registers of others, we appear to neglect more conventional forms of description and analysis. Yet by mimicking the forms and styles of local inscriptive and performative genres, the authors who adopt this strategy work toward not only more compelling, but also more complete, descriptions and analyses of the genres they research.

Choosing to use different narrative strategies, then, is not a fancy of the ethnographer, a muse that needs to be followed for her own sake. Nor is the work collected here meant to supplant other forms of writing ethnography, for each of us outside this volume continues to write within the recognized genre of our field. We have chosen to explore narrative possibilities here as one of many techniques we use in working to understand the lives and experiences of others. By writing ethnography that encompasses some of our own frailties, we begin to recognize the complexity of fixing culture in words. By attending specifically to narrative styles, we intend to amplify aspects of doing fieldwork that are otherwise barely audible. And by circulating these ethnographic outtakes, we strive to show ethnography as a creative process, constructed of ongoing conversations, hesitations, frustrations, and, inevitably, realizations.

In turning to these outtakes we are neither avoiding ethnographic truths nor covering up our own faulty memories. Rather, we hope that through these stories, some plausible and some perhaps less so, and through the different styles of telling them, that varied truths will unfurl in the midst of the looming muddle of writing about other people and places.

NOTES

1. This is not to say that Boas did not acknowledge his debt to Hunt. On the title page of his first major Kwakiutl ethnography, published in 1897, Boas specified that his report was "based on personal observations and on notes made by Mr. George Hunt" (1970 [1897], i) and acknowledges his debt to Hunt—"to whom I am under great obligations" (315)—in the first paragraph. In a later and shorter article, "The Social Organization of the Kwakiutl" (1920), Boas mentioned his correspondence with Hunt—which "clears up a number of points" (111)—also in the very first paragraph. For more on his Kwakiutl work, see Boas (1966); for more on his collaboration with George Hunt and his writing on shamanism, see Taussig (1998, 228–241).

2. See especially Marcus and Cushman (1982), Clifford and Marcus (1986), Marcus and Fischer (1986), and Clifford (1988). A number of provocative and useful explorations of the boundaries and possibilities of ethnographic representation have emerged since then. These include Trinh (1989), Fox (1991), Tedlock (1991), Thomas (1991), Krupat (1992), Okely and Callaway (1992), Lavie, Narayan, and Rosaldo (1993), Visweswaran (1994), Behar and Gordon (1995), Marcus (1998), Narayan (1989), and Russell (1999). A few recent ethnographies exploring these boundaries and possibilities are Abu-Lughod (1986), Kendall (1988), Narayan (1989), Kondo (1990), Behar (1993), Tsing (1993), Lortat-Jacob (1995), Stewart (1996), Lassiter (1998), and Emoff (2002). We do not mean to suggest that earlier authors did not address the aesthetic and political issues involved in doing and writing ethnography, for these questions most certainly have been with us from the early days of American anthropology. However, such issues clearly have become more prominent in recent writing about ethnography and more central to the practice of ethnography. As Barbara Tedlock noted in 1991, "There currently exists a new breed of ethnographer who is passionately interested in the coproduction of ethnographic knowledge, created and represented in the only way it can be, within an interactive Self/Other dialogue" (82). Her historical overview of the work that preceded the "emergence of narrative ethnography" actually suggests that this breed is not quite as new as it may seem, but there is no doubt that renewed concerns regarding the relations between culture, power, style, and representation have infused much ethnographic writing since the 1980s.

3. Mead's initial fieldwork in Papua New Guinea was published in 1939 in *From the South Seas: Studies of Adolescence and Sex in Primitive Societies.* Doubts about the validity of Mead's field research have spurred some anthropologists, as well as Samoans and Papua New Guineans, to question Mead's representational practices. Peter Worsley's early questioning of her limited field experience (1957) went largely unheard; Derek Freeman's 1983 criticism of Mead and the myth of Samoan promiscuity got much attention, but was roundly denounced. The afterword to Freeman's *The Fateful Hoaxing of Margaret Mead* (1999) summarizes the debate that his earlier work spawned. For more on Mead's work in

Papua New Guinea, see the film *Anthropology on Trial* (1983) and the book that emerged from that project (Foerstel and Gilliam 1992).
4. See, respectively but not exclusively, Clifford (1988), Marcus and Fischer (1986), Jackson (1995), and Torgovnick (1994).

REFERENCES

Abu-Lughod, Lila. 1986. *Veiled Sentiments: Honor and Poetry in a Bedouin Society.* Berkeley: University of California Press.

————. 1991. Writing against culture. In *Recapturing Anthropology: Working in the Present,* edited by Richard G. Fox, 137–162. Santa Fe: School of American Research Press.

Behar, Ruth. 1993. *Translated Woman: Crossing the Border with Esperanza's Story.* Boston: Beacon Press.

————. 1996. *The Vulnerable Observer: Anthropology That Breaks Your Heart.* Boston: Beacon Press.

Behar, Ruth, and Deborah Gordon, eds. 1995. *Women Writing Culture.* Berkeley: University of California Press.

Bhabha, Homi K. 1994. *The Location of Culture.* London and New York: Routledge.

Boas, Franz. 1920. The social organization of the Kwakiutl. *American Anthropologist* 22(2):111–126.

————. 1966. *Kwakiutl Ethnography,* edited by Helen Codere. Chicago: University of Chicago Press.

————. 1970 [1897]. *The Social Organization and the Secret Societies of the Kwakiutl Indians.* Landmarks in Anthropology Series, edited by Weston La Barre. New York: Johnson Reprint Corporation. Originally published in the *Annual Report of the National Museum* for 1895.

Carpenter, Edmund. 1974. *Oh, What a Blow That Phantom Gave Me!* Toronto, New York, and London: Bantam Books.

Clifford, James. 1988. *The Predicament of Culture.* Cambridge: Harvard University Press.

Clifford, James, and George E. Marcus, eds. 1986. *Writing Culture: The Poetics and Politics of Ethnography.* Berkeley: University of California Press.

Emoff, Ron. 2002. *Recollecting from the Past: Musical Practice and Spirit Possession on the East Coast of Madagascar.* Music/Culture Series. Middletown, CT: Wesleyan University Press.

Foerstel, Lenora, and Angela Gilliam, eds. 1992. *Confronting the Margaret Mead Legacy: Scholarship, Empire, and the South Pacific.* Philadelphia: Temple University Press.

Fox, Richard G., ed. 1991. *Recapturing Anthropology: Working in the Present.* Santa Fe: School of American Research Press.

Freeman, Derek. 1983. *Margaret Mead and Samoa: The Making and Unmaking of an Anthropological Myth.* Cambridge: Harvard University Press.

————. 1999. *The Fateful Hoaxing of Margaret Mead: A Historical Analysis of Her Samoan Research.* Boulder: Westview Press.

Jackson, Michael. 1995. *At Home in the World.* Durham, NC: Duke University Press.

Kendall, Laurel. 1988. *The Life and Hard Times of a Korean Shaman: On Tales and the Telling of Tales.* Honolulu: University of Hawaii Press.

Kondo, Dorinne K. 1990. *Crafting Selves: Power, Gender, and Discourses of Identity in a Japanese Workplace.* Chicago and London: University of Chicago Press.

Krupat, Arnold. 1992. *Ethnocriticism: Ethnography, History, Literature.* Berkeley: University of California Press.

Lassiter, Luke E. 1998. *The Power of Kiowa Song.* Tucson, AZ: University of Arizona Press.

Lavie, Smadar, Kirin Narayan, and Renato Rosaldo. 1993. *Creativity/Anthropology.* Ithaca, NY: Cornell University Press.

Lortat-Jacob, Bernard. 1995. *Sardinian Chronicles.* Chicago: University of Chicago Press.

Marcus, George E. 1998. *Ethnography through Thick and Thin.* Princeton, NJ: Princeton University Press.

Marcus, George E., and Dick Cushman. 1982. Ethnographies as texts. *Annual Review of Anthropology* 11:25–69.

Marcus, George E., and Michael M. J. Fischer. 1986. *Anthropology as Cultural Critique: An Experimental Moment in the Human Sciences.* Chicago: University of Chicago Press.

Mead, Margaret. 1939. *From the South Seas: Studies of Adolescence and Sex in Primitive Societies.* New York: William Morrow and Company.

Narayan, Kirin. 1989. *Storytellers, Saints, and Scoundrels: Folk Narrative in Hindu Religious Teaching.* Series in Contemporary Ethnography. Philadelphia: University of Pennsylvania Press.

Okely, Judith, and Helen Callaway, eds. 1992. *Anthropology and Autobiography.* London and New York: Routledge.

Russell, Catherine. 1999. *Experimental Ethnography: The Work of Film in the Age of Video.* Durham, NC: Duke University Press.

Stewart, Kathleen. 1996. *A Space on the Side of the Road: Cultural Poetics in an "Other" America.* Princeton, NJ: Princeton University Press.

Taussig, Michael. 1998. Viscerality, faith, and skepticism: Another theory of magic. In *In Near Ruins: Cultural Theory at the End of the Century,* edited by Nicholas B. Dirks, 221–256. Minneapolis: University of Minnesota Press.

Tedlock, Barbara. 1991. From participant observation to the observation of participation: The emergence of narrative ethnography. *Journal of Anthropological Research* 47(1):69–94.

Thomas, Nicholas. 1991. Against ethnography. *Cultural Anthropology* 6(3):306–322.

Torgovnick, Marianna, ed. 1994. *Eloquent Obsessions: Writing Cultural Criticism.* Durham, NC: Duke University Press.

Tsing, Anna Lowenhaupt. 1993. *In the Realm of the Diamond Queen: Marginality in an Out-of-the-way Place.* Princeton, NJ: Princeton University Press.

Trinh, Minh-ha T. 1989. *Woman, Native, Other: Writing Postcoloniality and Feminism.* Bloomington: Indiana University Press.

Visweswaran, Kamala. 1994. *Fictions of Feminist Ethnography.* Minneapolis: University of Minnesota Press.

WGBH. 1993. "Anthropology on Trial." *Nova.* Public Broadcast System. Boston: WGBH.

White, Jonathan. 1995. Coming back from the silence: An interview with Ursula K. Le Guin. *Whole Earth Review* no. 85:76.

Worsley, Peter. 1957. Margaret Mead: Science or Science Fiction?: Reflections of a British Anthropologist. *Science and Society* 21(2):122–134.

Samosir's Dark Rains

ANDREW CAUSEY

It's hard to say when the heavy rains really started to pour down out of the skies because it happened so gradually: first, gray shadows blocked the sun in the mornings as well as the afternoons, then low-slung and dark blankets of cloud dripped all day long. Finally, it rained. There was a steady rain for a day, and mist for a day; later it was just rain. The gutter-trench that surrounded my house, and supposedly drained the water that fell on the small hill in my backyard, puddled up white with mud water, then flowed translucent gray, then surged with water so quick and clear that it looked like glistening black glass. The gutter-trench could not drain the water from the hill quickly enough, however, and soon the path that connected me with Samosir Island's paved road, and with the rest of the village, was part of a wide, shallow pond. Now, my shoes were always wet because rain and pools of water were unavoidable.

The birds all seemed to have left the area. If they were still around, they were huddling, soggy, under forest leaves instead of darting in and out of the hedges and fields as they usually

Special thanks go to Amy Hawkins for her perceptive comments on this chapter.

did. The trills and arpeggios of yellow weaver birds and indigo
mynahs were gone. Now, the thick, damp air was filled with the
wheeze and croak of frogs in the new-formed pond or in the
black trench water. Some nights, when the rain let up and
became a sprinkle, their high-pitched creaking would drown
out all other nighttime sounds so effectively that I could not tell
if I what I heard was a seamless amphibian chord surrounded
by vibrating drizzle or just ringing in my ears. If the drench of
rain started up again, it only served to muffle their roar, not to
obliterate it. Almost everyone in the village went to bed early
on these drizzling nights because the sound of the TV could not
be heard over the constant thrilling of the frogs in the wet fields
and ponds in the village.

There was one night in the rainy season when I woke up
from a dream thinking I heard voices (and unworldly alien ones
at that) outside my house. When I came to some kind of consciousness, I realized it was the frogs outside making this crazy
noise, a kind of "grrrKEEK . . . grrrKEEK" sound over and over;
they did not stop even when, stumbling naked to the balcony
aching to sleep, I threw a few well-aimed rocks at their pond.

When the rains became persistent and regular, the smells on
Samosir Island dissipated like the birds' songs. Now, I only sensed
an occasional damp mildew, and even then, the scent was very
light: a whiff of some slight trace of something that was hard to
recall. My house was surrounded by a gardener's dream of hibis-
cus bushes, yellow gladiolus, and strange tropical plants with
glossy variegated leaves, and the soil in the fields next door was
constantly being plowed up with weeds turned upside-down and
left to rot, yet there was never a smell from any of this. I planted
a small garden at the base of my backyard hill, thinking that the
rains would make corn and radish seeds burst luxuriantly from
the ground. I picked up a handful of the sticky gray soil ready to
enjoy a deep nose-full of the humus, but there was no such
aroma. Then I sniffed harder. There, far below the sensation of
inhaling humidity, I caught a whiff of a very faint stink, something like a summer day's discovery that clothes were left too long

in the washer. Even the water buffalo shit didn't stink, and I know because I put my nose very close to it.

The rain came down dark and clear, especially in the evenings. The old fifty-gallon drum which collected my household water and which had been harboring only a few inches of velvety algae a few months before, was now always brimming with cold water. When the first thunderous storms glazed the roof in water, I would rouse myself at any hour of the night to fill the indoor cisterns. I carried bucket after bucket of cold rain against the wind and spray, guided by flickering candles indoors and a sooty kerosene torch outside. Now that it had been raining for so many weeks, however, I could not be roused from my covers. Every cistern, pail, and drum was filled; water surrounded me not only in flowing streams and still pools, but now in metal drums and covered pots.

During this time of constant rain, the days were sullen, people kept their umbrellas close to the door, and families spent their free time warming themselves inside the house. I lived in a huge concrete villa by myself, beyond the main cluster of houses in the village Huta Mungkap. During the first few nights of the wet season, I nursed myself with hot soup and cassette tapes, or with shots of a sweet liqueur I had bought on a whim in the city some months before. Such evenings of forced solitude were uncomfortably lonely for me. I read all of the novels I had brought to the island— long-winded narratives by Thomas Hardy and Umberto Eco— and when these were done, each word cherished and savored, I persuaded the tourists I met to trade their cast-off paperbacks with me. I encountered books by authors whose glories, printed in boldface on their covers, were written by critics from the *Riverside Tattler* or the *Charlotte Post-Register.* Some nights I wrote long letters home and followed this up by writing pages and pages of field notes. Occasionally, I crept into bed early, falling asleep to the scratchings and squabblings of field rats making their winter homes in the attic. While I usually got a lot done on the nights stuck at home, I felt cut off from the social whirl of the village, by the relentless, hammering downpours.

Whenever I thought my coat could deflect the rain, I would head over to the house of Partoho and Ito, my carving teacher and his wife. The smells of nature might have dissipated outside, but their kitchen was redolent with the scent of hot oils, wet children, and wood smoke. Many times I would walk the short mile to their house, holding my umbrella against a steady but soft shower, only to find myself holed up with them for hours as we waited out a cold tropical downpour. They always implored me to eat dinner with them when this happened, Ito calling out to me to sit down on the mat as she fried up some salted fish and chilis, or boiled some long green beans in coconut milk to go with the rice, the delicate scents of which would mingle with clove fumes as Partoho would invite me to join him in a *kretek* cigarette. After the enameled plates and aluminum bowls were carried off and the floor was swept of whatever crumbs the dogs did not find, the amber glasses of sweet tea were brought in and offered as dessert, and it was then that Partoho, Ito, and I would sit around chatting and weaving stories, watching the children fall asleep arrayed around us on the mat and holding in our thoughts and words when the sound of cloudbursts on the metal roof overwhelmed our small voices.

Partoho and Ito told me all sorts of things on these rainy nights. Sometimes they would tell me the history of village resentments and alliances, and other times they told me about the trouble with the exhausted soil and failed crops. The stories that began to concern me more and more were the ones about the spirits and ghosts that were said to be sharing the world with us on the island. Although Partoho and Ito are both Protestants (perhaps no more skeptical or less staunch in their beliefs than like-minded Christians in America), they, like many of their fellow Toba Bataks, blended a kind of practical animism into their beliefs. I myself am unsure about spirits: I *think* I know that I don't believe in phantoms and ghosts, but I am not sure. I have a strong urge to respect, yet soundly reject, the idea that essences or energies roam the earth and can influence human concerns. But for the brief time I was on the foreign territory of Samosir

Island, I decided I should consider all possibilities. This is why I listened attentively to their stories of spirits and made careful mental notes about which ones might act out against me and which would manifest themselves more simply, perhaps as a lingering hot touch on the skin.

I suppose I would not have been so concerned about the netherworld if it wasn't for the fact that everyone in Huta Mungkap talked about it so much: Christian beliefs are strong here, but so are beliefs in the existence of *begu*—ghosts. Once, when an evening rain was hammering against Partoho and Ito's metal roof, we heard something between an odd mousy squeak and a solid wooden "klok." All around me, the family's eyes got slightly larger with concern. Alarmed, I asked what kind of strange noise that was. Ito smiled and laughed theatrically while pulling her fabric up around her shoulders, telling me it was one of the dogs scratching to get in. "That's not what it sounded like," I said, but she continued pretending to scoff at the interruption, with some response like, "Oh, Andru, don't be so jumpy! There are no ghosts around here. Ha ha ha ha ha." Partoho was sanguine. His initial fright dissipated; he now sat next to me, puffing quietly on his clove cigarette. As Ito's feeble laughs faded, he looked over at me and said, "Andru, just remember, if you ever meet up with a *begu*, pick a bright green leaf and hold it between your index finger and thumb and walk home fast."

Over the months, Partoho told me that I could ward off certain *begu* by wearing a ring of white or yellow brass, "or if you can afford it, a silver ring with a green stone." He said the ghosts in the lake could be placated simply by being respectful of the nurturing water: bathe and wash with a good heart; fish with concentration; sail across the lake with serious thoughts. As we once sat carving under the eaves of his house, I asked him if there were any *begu* that could not be avoided. He hesitated a second then said, "Oh, sure. There is Begu Ganjang. It is really an evil *begu* that usually lives near deep streams or rivers. Actually, it can go anywhere at any time, but it especially likes to roam around when the rain is coming down slowly while the sun is still out. Have you ever looked around here when it is like that? No one is out. Everyone goes indoors because they are afraid." Begu Ganjang is tall, he told me, and nearly invisible. "If you meet this one, you would not see a body—just a head," he said. "And as you look up at it, its head goes as high as your eyes will go, rising up past the treetops."

Partoho told me that Begu Ganjang operates like this: if you are outside when the sun's rays light up the rain, you might feel a sharp and focused gust of wind hit you. You won't know what happened, but when you get home—*if* you have the time to get home—you will look at the skin that felt the wind and find it black and curdled. He looked at me seriously and said, "You die right away . . . you just fall over." Dogs know about Begu Ganjang too, and if it passes near them they will let out a long low howl; this is the only way to communicate their hollow terror before they are stricken.

The vivid image of Begu Ganjang reminded me to tell Partoho about the dream I had several nights before. It was clearer now: I had entered an old, derelict wooden house and went up steep stairs because above me I heard voices that wavered between mumbles and clear words. I went into a room lit up by a bright fog outside a window and saw five people, or rather five large heads propped on slender bodies dressed in soft, black cotton pajamas. When I entered the room, they came over to me, peering at me very closely and intently, all talking at once in voices that were both vague and abrupt, voices that sounded like robots . . . or frogs. "What do you think that means?" I asked Partoho. He shrugged and shook his head saying, "I don't know. Sometimes, if you hear a very clear voice—I mean one that comes in through your ears—it is your father trying to talk to you. But you tell of five people, five *begu,* so that seems different. If they seemed to want to pull your breath out or make you enter their circle, that is a different thing." I told him that they just came very close and talked; I got scared and ran off. We sat there under the eaves watching the misty drizzle which dripped from the roof not more than a foot away, making a border of small craters near our feet.

As he considered the facts I had presented to him, I stared at his jaw, his nostrils, his temples, waiting for an interpretation. As the smoke of his *kretek* rose up in the damp air, his profile was blurred. He finally said, "I think it was your father trying to chat with you in your dream."

The steadiness of Samosir's dark rains began to trap humid air inside my concrete house. I got used to the feeling of heavy and moist cotton shirts on my skin in the morning, but shuddered against the cool damp of my *kapok*-filled mattress at night. A month of chilly evenings passed before I tried to dry the cumbersome mattress one morning by airing it on the wide rear balcony. This balcony seemed to be my best option, not only because its dry wooden railings were built up on low walls (engineered, I suppose, to keep someone's babies from crawling off the edges), but also because it was protected from the sky by broad eaves. The door banged open as I wobbled the heavy pad out to the handrail for its day in the fresh air. Then I turned to go back indoors. I reached for the handle to pull the door behind me as I went in so that no additional humidity could enter the house and glimpsed a slim black slick at the door's top edge. I was startled to discover what appeared to be a knob of wet tar on the top of the door. The small hairs of the back of my neck seemed to shiver as I struggled to understand. Slowly raising myself up on my toes, I craned my neck forward, and my eyes widened in curious horror to find that the slippery black wedge of tar was in fact a tree frog crouching, just breathing, on its quiet perch in a notch on the top of the door. I did not know what to do. Not wanting to be near the glistening creature any longer than I had to, I stepped back into the house, gingerly closed and locked the door, and minced away, frantically shaking my hands as if this would rid me of the experience. There was something wrong (very wrong) about this encounter, but I was too upset to know what it might be. I went to my desk, sat down and stared at my small dark computer, clamped shut like a beached mollusk. As I rested there, casting my eyes around my papers and books, sorting out what I should do, I found myself grimacing and blinking, my hands resting upturned on my knees. My fragmented thoughts raced past, replaying the encounter over and over. Each time, the dread of the surprise of seeing something dark, slippery, and sinister increased. I finally regained some sort of composure by reminding myself of the wisdom learned in childhood: "The frog is more afraid of you than you are of it." Sighing heavily, I went downstairs. I would deal with the frog when it was time to bring the mattress back in from its airing.

Feeling ill at ease, I walked down to Partoho's workshop in the foggy drizzle. Even though my life in Huta Mungkap was relatively easy, I began to realize how emotionally draining it was to live in a place that was not home. Simple things confused me, and some of my most unexamined assumptions were hanging ragged and unprotected. "The other night Ito told me not to be jumpy," I thought. "Well, I *am* jumpy. Things are different here. This is not Texas." When I saw Partoho, I tried to hide my anxiety, but was betrayed by the tone in my voice as I told him about the frog. Reassuring and kind, he told me that this sort of frog, whether green or black, was of no concern. "It will just sit there quietly in the day, and in the night it will find bugs to eat," he said, "Nothing to worry about." I started carving a head from a piece of light-colored wood, but was distracted by dark thoughts and flashing images. After a cup of hot sweet tea with Partoho, I returned home.

The day on the porch did not seem to have much positive effect on my mattress, so I resolved to give in to its clammy touch. I also resolved, based on Partoho's advice, to leave the frog alone. After a few nights, I began to look forward to the damp bedding, the patter of rain on the metal roof, and the wheeling creak of frogs, for they became the prelude and incessant accompaniment to my exhausted, and ordinarily uninterrupted, slumber. One night, however, the tapping of the rain turned to a windy clatter, and then a deafening thrum. I had never heard the rain come down so hard and so long that it actually obscured the sound of the frogs. Wind battered the windows, jangling them in their frames, and bruised the doors against their latches. I wanted to see the brunt of this rain with my own eyes, so I threw the heavy sheets back and reached over to the bedside lamp. The electricity was dead. When I lit the nearby candle, it flickered in a breeze that came through the window panes, having trouble holding its fire. I madly searched for the flashlight and, thus armed, ran down the stairs, unlocked the back door, and stepped out onto the concrete slab where the cistern stood. The noise of the crashing rain seemed to vibrate my entire body, and rain was splashing out of the water drum in dramatic arcs. I was about to close the door, satisfied that I had seen the storm in its fury, but I saw a movement and stood frozen where I was. One of the gray pond toads hopped into the house. I had no time to scoot this unwelcome visitor out, for fast on his trail a viscous brown wave surged over the back door's threshold and over the floor of the kitchen and front room. The flood was very quiet and very quick, and I found myself ankle deep in cold, muddy water in only a few seconds. I hopped back up the stairs, leaving the frog to find its own solutions, and heard a new noise out on the balcony, an ominous gurgling sound beneath the roar of the rain.

Turning the knob of the balcony door, I was met with the full tilt of the gale-force winds. The door crashed open. It took only a moment to see that the low protective wall surrounding the balcony was acting as a basin and was rapidly filling up. The drainage holes had apparently become clogged with debris tossed around by the wind, and the brimming waters were already cresting the door's threshold. The bedroom floor was now covered in a fine film of glassy water. Desperately searching for a rod or stick to dislodge the clot in the porch drain, I spotted a wire coat hanger, and quickly twisted it open. I charged past my desk, my bent épée in hand, but stopped. Large drops were beginning to fall from the ceiling. Dripping slowly at first, they quickly began to multiply exponentially. I heaved the stacks of papers and letters, notes and books, computer and printer onto the bed—the only place the ceiling's shower had not yet touched. I had never been in the attic before, since I felt I had deeded it over to the rodents for the rainy season, but now I began throwing together a scaffolding of wooden chairs on the desk to reach the crawl hole before everything I owned became drenched in filthy, ratty water. Wavering on the swaying chairs, I pushed the slatted door up, struggled past the first rush of gathered water, and saw a louvered ventilation window standing brightly open at a slant, accepting all available rain as if with open arms. I knocked past old naugahide suitcases and sagging cardboard boxes to crank the window shut, then hopped back down to the desk. Now, with my wire sword, I ran to unclog the drain.

A few deft pokes were enough. The weight of the accumulated water forced the sticks and leaves out in a splattering rush onto the ground below. Although the rain had not let up, the threat of an upstairs flood was now averted. Pulling hard against the wind, I closed the balcony door tightly shut, locking it with difficulty and shoving rags in the bottom cracks. The storm subsided slightly over the next hours as I mopped and wiped and swept the floors, then fell into an aching sleep on the damp sheets with my notes and books surrounding me. The house lulled me to sleep with its creaks and moans as the winds trudged their way south.

In the morning, I surveyed the damage: curling papers, a few warped books, a thin coat of mud on the floor upstairs and a thick layer of silt downstairs. Stepping outside, I found that the frog pond had become an ocean of churned-up water and murk. The morning sky was overcast but lighter than it had been for some days. I cut a trench from the pond to my neighbor's rice field and watched it move slowly downhill. The village was in a stir, everyone chattering excitedly about where they were when the storm hit, how they shouldered the doors against the floods, when there had last been such a tempest. My story vied with the best of them, but after an hour or so, there seemed to be nothing left for anyone to say; no one was hurt and no permanent damage was done. So, the daily pattern of the village returned: young boys towed the water buffaloes to graze, blacksmiths fanned the red embers, women sifted the rice, and shop owners flung open doors and windows. I wandered down to Partoho's house to continue carving the head I had started earlier.

The rains continued for weeks, and although they were mild compared with the great storm, they still caused the house to retain its musty smell. I waited patiently for the first rain-free day, the day I planned to hang out the sheets and blankets on the windy, uncovered balcony, the day I could open all the windows and doors to blow some of the humid funk out and away. As the days passed, so did the relentlessness of the rain. Each gentle break in the clouds, when a soft and light phrase of blue became visible amidst the grey, lightened my mood. The transformation of the sky was subtle yet noticeable.

When the first sunny, bright day finally arrived, I found that all of the house's frames and jambs were swollen shut. The porch door was particularly hard to open, requiring a sharp blow to loosen it. And another. The door swung open slowly, making a brittle, cracking sound. I looked up to see where the sound had come from and saw a tiny arm hanging loose from edge of the jamb. I leaned closer, my shoulders hunched in horrified curiosity. There, flattened on the inside frame of the door, was the rest of the body: a tiny humanoid with skin like soot, its remaining arm gracefully gesturing to the heavens, its head twisted back, and its legs in graceful, dancing arcs. I was bewildered and stunned to see this mummified homunculus crushed into the frame of the door. Mesmerized by the sight, I slowly shifted my gaze to a disciplined line of tiny black ants working from the creature's back. The world around me went out of focus. With each of my heartbeats, the flattened body crawling with bugs seemed to become magnified. "*BEGU!*" I screamed. "*BEGU! BEGU!*" I slammed the door. I was scared and revolted, but transfixed. "A rotting devil . . . crushed in door!" my mind screamed, "What will I *do*?!" Once again I went into involuntary grimacing and hand shaking, but this time I did not want to rationalize the experience. I raced over to Partoho's.

On my one-minded jog to his house, passing through the village deaf to its sounds, only vaguely conscious of its houses and people, I was flooded with images and emotions. I came to understand that I had accepted the reality of spirits and ghosts in this land and had given in to my primal fear of them. "This is not Texas," I reminded myself. "Weird things happen here."

Finding Partoho carving indoors, I blurted the whole story out to him: door; devil; fear. Although he quietly listened to the elaborate tale, he also shook his head during the entire recital. This made me both speed up the narrative and truncate some parts to keep his attention. At my first hesitation he said, "*Begu* cannot get crushed in a door, Andru." Wide-eyed, I shook my head rapidly and told him I *knew* that the black dwarf creature was a *begu,* but he went on, "*Begu* are not eaten up by ants, Andru. *Begu* are not black and do not die. They are dark and smoke-like, and they can kill with a breath. Since you are not dead, Andru, that thing in your door is no *begu.*" I felt betrayed by my teacher. "How can you know if it is a *begu* or not if you don't come see it?" I pleaded. He remained silent, continuing to shake his head.

"If it is not a *begu,* it is an *iblis,* a satan . . . a devil!" I cried out, trying to convince him. At this, he just laughed. Now the preposterousness of a devil captured in something so mundane as a doorjamb seemed slightly funny to me, too, but I blushingly suppressed my smile. Over the next hour, Partoho would give me frequent sidelong glances, each time chuckling. My pride shrank a notch each time.

I did not go home to check on the devil right away. I stayed at Partoho's house, chatting with him about other things, hoping that the image of my ranting about a squashed devil would dissipate in his mind. Once on my way, I walked home as quickly as I could. Upstairs, I delicately opened the porch door to see what was there. The ants were still at work, and now I could see parts of a pearly skeleton. I forced myself to look closer at the disfigured thing and saw, as Partoho had perhaps already guessed, that these bones and skin were the last remains of the black tree frog.

Composed now, I could reconstruct the event: the wind of the storm, jarring the frog loose from its safe aerie, forced it to cling to the doorjamb, a place of temporary refuge until I pulled the door shut against it. "What a sad way to leave the world," I thought and closed the door again. I made a decision to keep the door closed until the ants were done, not necessarily out of respect for the innocent black frog, but out of an aversion to dealing with dead and decaying things. Months later, when sunny days were regular and predictable, I opened the door to let light and air in. I searched the jamb, but found that the crepe-like skin and delicate porcelain bones had vanished. It seemed incomprehensible to me that hard bones (fine and twiglike though they were) could simply disappear. There was no trace of an outline of the creature, nor was there any dust at the base of the jamb; the paint of the door frame was not marred and its wood not dented. Now that there was nothing left of it, I anxiously wondered how to ask Partoho if frogs could become *begu.*

Sacred Secrets: Lessons with Francisco

KATHERINE J. HAGEDORN

When I ask Francisco questions about a drum pattern he is teaching me for one of the *santos,* he often says, "Is secret." Or "Is sacred." Or something in between. I can't tell what he's saying all the time because I don't always understand him. He speaks in the margins between Spanish and English. Sometimes he'll begin the lesson with, "OK, Katalin, vamos a hablar en español." But within ten minutes he's back to speaking in the margins, stubbornly pushing out words and phrases into a language that only he understands completely. And it's not as though I don't speak Spanish—I do. It's just that I don't speak Spanish like a Cuban from Matanzas who moved to the United States in the 1950s. Whenever we converse in "his" and "my" Spanish, he invariably says to me, "How come you speak Spanish so good, Katalin? You sound like a schoolteacher." And then he goes back to Francisco-speak, as if his Spanish and my own don't mix, or can't communicate, so he is forced to dip into his own special linguistic cache.

I've known Francisco for almost seven years now. I met him a few months after I finished my dissertation, in June 1995, at the house of a shady and very rich lawyer in Beverly Hills, who was also Francisco's long-time friend. I was there with three colleagues, Raul, Nancy, and Anthony, who were interviewing Francisco for the Smithsonian Institution's Jazz Oral History Program. This particular interview was part of a series focusing on renowned Latino jazz drummers, including Patato Valdés, and Mongo Santamaría; and Armando Peraza-Francisco certainly fit in. He used to perform regularly with Dizzy Gillespie and Frank Sinatra when they were alive and had long-standing gigs with the late Peggy Lee and the late Tito Puente. He did shorter tours with many other jazz musicians, great and small, and in the early 1990s began performing and touring in earnest with his own Latin Jazz Ensemble. He occasionally got into fist-fights with some of his musicians on stage during a show, which earned him something of a reputation. All of this came out in the interview—eventually.

I say "eventually" because there was that language problem again. Raul, who was running the interview, spoke to Francisco in Spanish, but even Raul's Cuban Spanish wasn't quite the same brand as Francisco's. Raul grew up on the other side of the island, in Santiago, hundreds of miles from Matanzas, and the accent is different. Although he and Francisco understood each other much better than Francisco and I did, there were still a few dull pauses, followed by "Say what?" or "Es what?" or "Say qué?" or "Ese qué?" or something like that. And Raul would repeat the question, which sometimes elicited the same response. Gradually we became aware of the possibility that Francisco might not hear very well. So we spoke more loudly, and this helped. And then I got over my nervousness about asking questions and learned to make them shorter and louder, which also helped. By the end of the interview, we had established a good rapport; but the end of the interview was, well, the end of the interview, and a good rapport seemed superfluous.

We were getting ready to leave the posh house in Beverly Hills on the last day of the interview. The large-screen television in the living room reflected the water in the large tiled pool outside. As morning flattened out into afternoon, the large mahogany antiques and plush Turkish carpets swelled in the center of this triangle of light. I felt drowsy and warm, not quite ready to leave. Spurred to action by our impending departure, I asked Francisco (in English) whether he would consider giving me drum lessons. He said, "Lemme see if you got ritmo," and handed me an *okónkolo* (the smallest of a set of three double-headed Cuban *batá* drums). He gave me a basic rhythm to play, ki-ha, ki-ha, ki-ha, and told me to "keep it up." Then he proceeded to play a few drum calls on the *iyá* (the largest and most talkative of the three *batá* drums), simply at first, and then gradually filling out the basic rhythmic structures as he gauged my interest and ability. After about two minutes he began "stealing time," improvising in tricky and distracting ways, to see whether I would lose the beat. The *okónkolo* and I held our ground (which felt like maintaining a steady pattern while the walls shook and the earth opened up), and he said, to no one in particular, "Eh, mira! She got ritmo!"

Raul acted as the intermediary (the three of us met at Porto's Cuban bakery in Glendale to discuss the details), and within a couple of months I began lessons with Francisco. I was very happy about taking lessons from this master drummer, but also nervous. I had heard stories about his gruff manner and limited patience and was anxious to be a good student. Francisco had agreed to give me lessons in any Cuban drumming tradition I wanted—*conga, rumba, iyesa, palo, batá;* he had been playing them all since his teens in Matanzas in the late 1930s and 1940s. I chose lessons on the *batá* drums, the double-headed set of three wooden drums used mostly in the ceremonies of the Afro-Cuban religious tradition known as Santería. Although Francisco had successfully skirted his deep musico-religious responsibility to Santería for almost forty years, he finally became an *omí añá* in 1980. *Omí añá* literally means "child of the drum," a title bestowed upon those drummers who become initiated into *añá,* or the drumming *oricha* (another word for *santo,* or deity), so that they can communicate with the other *santos* in Santería. Since then, Francisco has played for *toques de santo,* Santería drumming ceremonies in honor of initiations, saints' days, and other religious events) in Los Angeles, San Francisco, and everywhere in between. He is considered an expert *batá* drummer with limitless stamina.

I chose *batá* lessons with Francisco because I felt that knowing more about *batá* rhythms would help my research into Afro-Cuban religious and folkloric performance in Cuba. My first lessons on the *batá* drums had taken place in Havana, in the early 1990s, with Alberto, the lead drummer for the Cuban National Folkloric Ensemble. I had worked hard to get him to teach me (he rejected my initial requests because, he said, I "played like a girl") and had worked even harder to establish a solid repertoire of Havana-style *batá* patterns. But establishing a solid repertoire of patterns is not the same as knowing the structures of the calls among the *iyá, itótele,* and *okónkolo* and knowing how and when to improvise. Most good *batá* drummers study and play for at least a couple of years with "master" drummers before they consider themselves truly competent to play with other drummers in a folkloric or ritual context. I wanted to become a competent drummer, so I seized the opportunity to continue my studies with someone closer to home.

For the first few months, Francisco and I shared the commute: sometimes he would come out to my house in Claremont (forty miles east of downtown Los Angeles), and sometimes I would travel to his house in Echo Park, on the outskirts of the city. Each lesson was two hours long, with Francisco beating out specific patterns on a drum, and me trying to imitate them. Francisco would speak during these early lessons only to reprimand me for playing a rhythm incorrectly. "No!" Then he would play the pattern again, at the same tempo, but louder. I would usually pick it up the second time he played it, after which he would sometimes give an almost imperceptible nod of approval. If I didn't get the rhythm after the second time, he would play the same pattern even more loudly. Asking for an explanation of what was incorrect about my rendition of the rhythm proved to be futile. His response to that category of questioning was simply to play the rhythm again and again: I was to learn by listening not to his words, but to his playing. In this sense, our lessons were stark, direct matters: drum pattern, painstaking imitation, short reprimand, repeat—with one exception.

The one exception was the muttering of endearments that would follow the rare encouraging remark. "Thass good, Katalin! You got it, Toyota Coroña! (now muttering) Oh you so smart, so beautiful, oh *mami* . . ." (Didn't he mean Toyota Corona?) I didn't catch all of these endearments at first, but my ears pricked up at "mami," a word usually reserved by Puerto Rican, Cuban, and other Latino Caribbean men for their wives, girlfriends, or objects of affection. "Please don't call me *mami,* Francisco. I'm not your girlfriend." But the endearments continued, intensifying when Francisco would grasp and move my hands to emphasize the correct way to hit the *batá* drum(s). Then his hands would rest longer than necessary on my wrists or arms after he finished showing me a particular drum stroke, or they would travel upward, just past my elbows, and squeeze the beginning of my biceps and triceps. "Ooooh, you strong, Katalin! You born to be *batalera.*" Each time he violated my physical space, I would tell him to stop. Sometimes he would desist, but more often he would act as though he hadn't heard me. Dreading these confrontations, I would avoid these physically intimate moments with him whenever possible by generating spontaneous mini-dramas: I would tell him to show me the drum pattern and hand position from the front rather than from the back (so that he would face me, and the drum would separate us), I would sneeze at a propitious time (causing him to jump back), I would almost drop a drum on the floor (dramatically twisting away from him to catch it), I would get up abruptly to go to the bathroom in the middle of a rhythm (pushing him out of the way with my drum), etc. But as the year progressed these scenes grew increasingly uncomfortable and frequent. After one lesson, he blocked me from opening the door as he was leaving, and then grabbed the back of my neck and tried to stick his tongue down my throat. I twisted away from his grip, gasping, and shouted at him to get out. "You mad at me, Katalin?" "Yes, I'm mad at you. You just stuck your tongue down my throat. Get out!" "OK, OK Katalin. I can't help it. When you not gonna be mad anymore?" "I don't know."

After a month, I had decided to continue my lessons with him. Even as I was angry with him, I remained fond of him. There was something both hideous and hilarious about his inappropriate pursuit of me during our lessons. He is more than seventy-five years old, yet oddly childish in some ways. And his stated preferences for women (which he continually shared with me during our lessons) always included the blonde and the buxom, of which I am neither. The fact that I am roughly half his age just made the situation more absurd and made it more difficult for me to interpret his advances as wholly threatening. I called him to reinstate our lesson schedule and to negotiate clearer boundaries about appropriate behavior.

The transgressive gestures did not stop altogether, but they greatly diminished, and I responded to these less than ideal conditions during my lessons with concise reprimands of my own. "No!" "Stop it!" Sometimes these felt like the barked-out commands of a drill sergeant, and it was difficult to square my reprimands with the awe and reverence I felt for the *conga* and *batá* performances of this master drummer. But in the same way that he was both an accomplished septuagenarian drummer and an unpredictable social participant, I was both his student and a professor of ethnomusicology, and I did not tolerate well the erosion of trust in this student–teacher relationship.

By this time, I had stopped driving to Echo Park, where some of the more egregious physical transgressions had occurred. Instead, Francisco traveled to Claremont each week for the lessons. He liked my house, he said, and felt comfortable drumming in the large front room. "You neighbors? They not gonna call the police?" "No, Francisco. It's fine." Every few weeks he would ask, "You wanna trade?" And I would respond, "Trade what?" He would laugh, and blurt out, "Trade house! You take my house, I take your house. OK?" It was during these lessons in 1996 that he first began talking about sacred/secrets and asking me whether I wanted to be a Santera (priestess of Santería). This series of exchanges started when I asked him to tell me the meaning of the words to a song for *Ogún* (a warrior *santo* in Santería) that he said his grandmother sang. ("Ogún dere arere, ile bombo, Ogúa, Ogún wanile, Ogún walona, ile bombo Ogú aye.") "Is sacred [secret]." "Secret?" I asked. "Sacred [secret], secret [sacred]," he responded. "Why is it sacred? Or a secret?" "Is sacred [secret]" was once again his response. Every time I would ask a question about the meaning of a text, or why a particular rhythm was played for a particular *santo*, or any specific question referring to the meaning or context of Santería performance, Francisco would give me the sacred/secret response. Even when I would rephrase the question in Spanish, hoping for clarification, Francisco would answer me in his mixed argot, cheerfully stonewalling my careful attempts to decipher his linguistic code.

A friend of mine hypothesized that Francisco responded that way when he didn't know the answer to my questions. I thought about this explanation for several weeks, and it both disturbed and amused me. Was it really possible that someone who had been involved in this performance tradition for all but about fifteen years of his long life could know "nothing" about its meaning and context? Or was it more likely that the sacred/secret response was a roadblock, meant to dissuade the uninitiated traveler? I weighed the former possibility against my need for Francisco to know the things I wanted him to know. (What a fieldwork charade that would be—investing years of energy and money into lessons from a "master drummer," who knows the strokes, but nothing else.) I clung to the idea that his mastering of the tradition included a good deal of knowledge about and interest in the context of its performance. I could understand him not wanting to tell me about it, but I could not accept the possibility that he might not know it. (How could he not know, or not want to know?) Eventually, my sense of the absurd got the better of me, and I confronted Francisco with the possibility that he was using the sacred/secret strategy to cover up gaps in his knowledge. He responded by looking at me quizzically and asking, "Say qué?"

Twice more I tried to explain my doubts about sacred/secrets, and twice more he responded, "Ese what?" "Ese qué?"

During a particularly difficult passage in the *itótele* rhythm for Yemayá, I asked Francisco what Yemayá's rhythms "meant." After the usual round of "Say qué?" he put down his *iyá* drum and leaned toward me, his elbows resting on his knees. "Why you wanna know this stuff?" I was surprised at this apparently straightforward (and long-awaited) response to my persistent questioning. "Because I'm deeply interested in it. The music affects me—here." I tapped the central point of my solar plexus. "You wanna be Santera?" he asked. "Because you askin' questions like you wanna be Santera." I asked him whether only [Santeras] could know the answers to the questions I was asking. He chuckled and picked up the *iyá* again, shaking his head. "You gonna be Santera. Katalin gonna be Santera." He repeated "Katalin gonna be Santera" in a sing-song voice several times, and continued chuckling. I put down the *itótele* and told him I was not ready to be a Santera; I only wanted to know the answers to these questions because the music had such a powerful effect on me. Again he engaged me, but only briefly. "The music powerful because the *santo* make it powerful. The music is the *santo*."

We took a break in our lessons for a couple of months during the summer, and when we started lessons again in August 1996, I told him I was planning to go back to Cuba in 1997. He said, "You goin', just you?" He was thinking of going to Cuba, too, but didn't know when. This would have been the first time he would have returned to Cuba in almost 45 years, after he had left in the early 1950s to go on tour with the Katherine Dunham Dance Troupe. It was in the fall of 1996 that he started talking to me about getting "processed." He pronounced the word with the emphasis on the "cess," and with a slight voicing of the "ed." I asked him when a particular song for Eleguá ("A ri di di di de, Eshu Odara, di de oku olona, a ri di di di de . . .") would typically be performed. "When the people they get processed in the *santo*" was the answer. "Processed?" I asked. "In what way?" "The way the *santo* processes the people!" he replied. "Katalin, you gotta get processed. Then you know." *Santo* processing? Like food processing? Or processing applications from prospective initiates? It took a few minutes for my mind to introduce "processed" to "possessed," and for the two words to look each other over and agree to be temporarily interchangeable. "Possessed?" I asked. "Processed! Processed!" he nodded vehemently.

I went to Cuba in July of 1997 and delivered a letter and some money to Francisco's sister in Matanzas. She wrote back to Francisco that now more than ever she wanted him to visit her, that neither of them was getting any younger. She also allowed that she wouldn't mind taking the flight to Los Angeles, either. I passed on his sister's messages to him, as well as greetings from the extended family in Matanzas. Francisco became thoughtful and repeated that he might go back to Cuba within the year. We started our lessons again that fall, and his responses to my questions gradually filled in some of the stubborn gray silences of the unutterable sacred/secrets. Now he was including sly signs, passwords into his worldview, so that the sacred/secrets might be not only possessed, but processed. During one lesson Francisco talked about the "procession" of an initiate by Shangó at a *toque de santo* the previous weekend. It became clear from the context of our conversation that he was referring to what I would call *oricha* possession, but he kept using the word "procession" to describe it. My mind transformed the *toque* into a graduation ceremony, in which the possessed initiate processed jauntily across the room to the calls of the *batá* drums, *santo* diploma in hand, his red gown and matching cap bouncing to and fro, while appreciative onlookers processed the scene.

As we continued our lessons over the next year, Francisco's career was on the upswing. Les Blank's documentary film about Francisco's life as a drummer, *Sworn to the Drum,* gave him more exposure, and two record companies were interested in reissuing his old albums on CDs, as well as signing him up to make new recordings. As Francisco had predicted, I was becoming more involved in Santería through my fieldwork in Cuba, gradually completing the various phases of initiation. We saw less of each other during the spring of 1998 because of busy schedules, and I moved up to San Francisco for my academic leave, from June 1998 through June 1999. During the fall of 1998 Francisco came up to San Francisco three times, twice to give me lessons, and once for a gig at Mr. E's, a club in downtown Berkeley. On each day of these three-day visits, we would meet for a couple of hours for a lesson and then go out for a meal, during which we would discuss the lesson and sometimes Santería in general.

It was during that fall that Francisco got to know my husband, Peter, and tried to explain to him the importance of "the *santo*." I had returned from another trip to Cuba at the end of September 1998, during which I had completed my initiation into *Santería,* and Francisco had come up from Los Angeles for a lesson a few weeks later. We had just had a lesson, and the three of us were sitting in the living room drinking coffee. Peter and I had *café cubano;* Francisco preferred *café americano* with lots of milk. Francisco saw my small altar and remarked that the *santo* was powerful. Peter asked what made the *santo* so powerful, and Francisco offered one of his rare stories as an explanation. "This one guy, he had hands like baseball glove. Go to the doctor, doctor don't know. He can't do nothin' with his hands. He wanna play music, can't play. He wanna write, can't write. He go to another doctor, can't do nothin'. His friend he say, 'Go to Santero, maybe Santero can help.' He go, and Santero say give food to the *santo* and the *santo* will help. He do it, and the next day—true!—that guy his hands fine! He do everythin' like a normal person! Now he believe in the *santo* a lot. He have altar, party for the *santo,* everythin'."

We all nodded appreciatively at this strange and miraculous story. The *santo* was truly powerful. The story left us with little else to say. After an extended pause, I asked about our dinner plans, which led to a discussion of food taboos in Santería. Francisco volunteered a tale of a man who had ignored the food taboos communicated to him by his *santo.* "His *santo* say he not supposed to eat red beans. But that guy he like red beans, so he eat them. And then all sudden red beans come out his eyes, his ears, his mouth, his nose. And he get sick! Real sick! The *santo* is a mischief, big

big mischierf." I transcribe the word here as "mischierf"; it sounded like something in between "mischief" and "mystery." I asked, "The *santo* makes mischief?" Francisco nodded vigorously. "The *santo* is a big mystery?" He nodded again. "Yes—big big mischierf!" "You mean, like, mysterious? Unpredictable? Unknown?" He clapped his hands together. "Ver mischierious." I persisted. "Or sort of like playing tricks on someone?" "Yes, big mischierf." The word remained somewhere in between "mischievous" and "mysterious," tricky and unknown.

That evening the three of us went to La Rondalla, a nearby Mexican restaurant, for dinner, and Peter asked how the *santos* know which *batá* rhythms to respond to. Francisco said that any rhythm could bring down any *santo*. The *santo*, he added, sometimes gets lonely. After "processing" someone, the *santo* might grab another person to make that person get processed by a different *santo*, who will keep the first *santo* company. However, he said, sometimes the people aren't strong enough to get processed by the *santo*, so they just get "checkup" instead. I thought "checkup" might be "shake[n] up," which could refer to the shaking and convulsing that occurs when someone is in the initial throes of *oricha* possession but can't quite succumb to the *santo*. But the idea of a *santo* "checkup" intrigued me. "So the *santo* checks up on the person?" I asked. "Yeah, the *santo* checkup the person." "You mean shake up, as in convulsing? Or checkup, like at the doctor's office?" "Checkup! Checkup! You can do it at a doctor's office, but most people they don't."

These exchanges were by turns frustrating and funny, because they never seemed to ease my difficulties in understanding him, yet they always provided another (often humorous) perspective from which to consider my original question. Francisco's "answer" was never one or the other choice, but the same, stubborn, in-between combination of the two choices, which seemed to leave me stranded at the (crossroads) of not-quite-understanding. Or did it? The repetition of the words, much like the repetition of the drumming patterns, implied that I wasn't getting it, that I needed to listen more carefully to what he was saying and playing. This required patience, at the very least, and faith in the possibility that the key to his message lay hidden in a performative detail, which I could apprehend if I just listened carefully. There was also the possibility that Francisco shuffled and obscured pronunciations of certain words on purpose, as a truly intimate form of entertainment—at my expense. And that maybe, if I were a more alert field researcher and student, I would be able to decode his signals, or at least establish a rapport with him that would encourage a more forthcoming, even effusive, linguistic relationship.

But the unavoidable fact is that Francisco speaks in the margins, somewhere between Matanzas Spanish and Los Angeles English, so it is futile to try to make his words fit into one or the other lexical mold. It is unjust and inaccurate to assume that Francisco cannot pronounce certain words and therefore cannot fully grasp their meaning. What seems more likely is that he is creating a new language, a personal creole, in which his syntax and lexicon communicate a world beyond the words and meanings of "procession" and "possession" as we know them, yet also include them: a fusion of pronunciations signifying a fusion of meanings. We all engage in this private poetry to some extent, but the results of Francisco's creations seem both more evocative and more elusive to me because he uses his adopted English tongue as the surface structure for his improvisations.

The idea of a personal creole intrigues me because it admits the possibility of deep semantic play in a "second" language, and because it provides the opportunity to explore resulting underground passages of homophonic ambiguity. In Santería performance traditions, secrets are sacred, and, conversely, sacred aspects of performance are secret. One can only "know" them by performing them, and one can only perform them by being initiated into Santería. Since I was not initiated into Santería at the time of the sacred/secret exchanges, I was not likely to get to know these performative aspects of Santería, by performance or otherwise. Moreover, because *batá* drumming in religious contexts is only performed by initiated men, not women, it was unlikely that I would ever come to know the "sacred/secrets" of *batá* drumming by performing them. The "sacred/secret" response both impeded my understanding and implied the possibility of additional knowledge through initiation.

"Process/possess" may have been another form of cognitive shorthand. Possession is indeed a process, a state of being that is approached gradually, sometimes over a period of years. Most people cannot simply give themselves over to the spirit of a deity or an ancestor at the first sign of that entity's presence. The first manifestations of possession—such as a sharp tingling in the fingers and toes, sudden dizziness, sobbing and swaying, or involuntary jerking and shaking—are so alarming that one's first response is typically to fight against the invading force, to regain a previous state of relative equilibrium. One learns how to become possessed through the process of possession, in a way similar to that in which one learns to meditate through the process of meditation. I have never allowed myself to become fully possessed (the prospect is still too scary for me), and I am too "young" in the religion to be very adept at it. So when Francisco said to me that I needed to be "processed" to know what it meant, perhaps he was referring literally to the "possession process," the "process" of learning to be "possessed," and the "processing" of my consciousness through the tropes and symbols of Santería "possession."

The *santos* in Cuban Santería are often referred to as "mysteries," but the only deity who routinely evokes "mischief" is Eleguá-Echu, the trickster deity of the crossroads. The *santos* as "big, big mischierf" is a telling trope. (What reason have they to be "good" all the time? Why not create a little mischief on the side, especially if they are as anthropomorphic as many scholars and practitioners of Santería would have us believe?) Certain roads (or aspects) of particular *santos* are indeed mischievous, if not downright ferocious (for example, most roads of Babalú-Ayé, the deity of infirmity and disease; the roads of Ogún Echibirikí, who is the most ferocious of all the Ogúns, the primary warrior deity; and Echu Agganiká, Echu Akileyó, Echu Akokelebiyú, etc., all of whom are roads of Eleguá-Echu). What makes the divine manifestations of these roads mischievous is their unpredictability and occasional malice, combined with the disturbing fact that humans cannot always placate them. The *santo* as "big mischierf"—"mischief" and "mystery" combined— points to the awesome, arbitrary power of the divine: pure *aché*, the theological crux in Santería that is the power to make things— anything—happen.

With this in mind, it is no wonder that devotees of Santería sometimes get "checkup." The very thought of being "processed" by one of these *santos* is indeed a "big mischierf," invoking a "checkup" of the most serious kind. In Francisco's message to me about the *santo* "checking up" the person, he leaves out the preposition "on," which implies that the *santo*'s action is much more agitative than simply looking in on someone. "Checking up" on the person becomes combined with "shaking up" the person, so that "procession" is both a physical and a spiritual checkup. ("You can do it at a doctor's office," said Francisco, "but most people they don't.") Most people put off doctor's appointments (who likes to go to the doctor's office?), and most people would not want to get "processed" or "checkup" in the doctor's waiting room, either. One can't necessarily control a *santo* "check-up," which manifests as a shaking up of the devotee ("Listen to me! I want to come in!") and which, understandably, leaves the acolyte "shaked up."

These word blurs seem to me to be a way of marking boundaries, even as they defy conventional semantic categories. I ask Francisco questions about sensitive matters, issues that cannot necessarily be generalized under the category of "information." Rather, my questions delve into the realm of personal religious conviction, where generalities convey but a pale approximation of meaning. Francisco answers my questions in the only way that he can—with phrases that imply other worlds without unmasking them, with words that fuse together cultures without diminishing them, and with an accent that allows him to offer slivers of experience without divulging their origins. His goal, then, is to protect the sacred secrets, to guard the mischievous and mysterious possession process, without getting too shaked up about it—you got it, Toyota Corona.

Wildness in the Heart of Town

RON EMOFF

A pervasive odor enshrouds the streets of Antananarivo, the capital of Madagascar—a combination of lead gasoline combustion, burning hardwood (which Malagasy people use for cooking), and rotting human defecation. This odor is at first both repugnant and engaging, such a powerful olfactory sensation, even a slight burn in the back of the throat, that one can almost imagine it into being much later. At the muddy *taxi-brousse* station in Antananarivo, a light early-morning rain was concentrating this odor and drizzling it onto the bodies of Malagasy people waiting to spend long cramped hours in travel. One young Malagasy man had a stringed instrument in one hand. He stood patiently waiting for his ride, unconcerned that droplets of rain were settling on his rather unusual-looking instrument.

The instrument's wooden body had been carved delicately into the form of a portable radio–cassette player, detailed with carrying handle; fast forward, reverse, and play buttons; radio frequency and volume control knobs; frequency band display; condenser microphone; and speaker—a striking image of aural empowerment. Radio transmissions in Madagascar often originate from the Malagasy National Radio Station. Was this musician empowering himself iconically with the broadcast of his own playing over the national radio frequency, imagining himself into national musical recognition? Perhaps this instrument's mimetic form had been designed to convey criticism over the *unlikelihood* that one's own music would ever be nationally recognized, or over the (in)accessibility in Madagascar of actual radio–cassette players, which are often prohibitively expensive.

I had been in Antananarivo for the past three and a half weeks, waiting to be issued a long-term research visa. I was finally heading for Tamatave, a bustling port town on the east coast of the island, where I would spend most of the next two years. Previously I had only dreamed of the Indian Ocean—an eternal expanse of blue green, with a swollen moon perched on the horizon and reflecting erratically below on yellow bobbing crests. Yet any of my delight with finally arriving in Madagascar was necessarily tinged with ambivalence. For one, very young Malagasy children swathed in filthy rags were always begging for change from *vazaha* (white outsiders) in the dirty, bumper-to-bumper Antananarivo streets. And there was talk everywhere of the environmental devastation widespread throughout Madagascar, which leaves considerably less arable land each year on which to grow rice. Then there were the dire national economic problems and the powerlessness of the current president to do much about them. This was a strange, inequitable, disturbing awakening. I was intensely charged by this world of difference—as if I were learning all over again how food tastes, colors radiate, music sounds— while Malagasy people themselves had to maneuver so tenaciously to survive in this same world.

The man with the stringed instrument seemed to notice my visual fascination with it, though he said nothing to me. Another Malagasy man leaned toward me and said in French that this musician was Antandroy, from the south of the island. To my puzzlement he added, shaking a finger at me, "Faites attention!" The instrument man, who apparently spoke no French, smiled placidly in my direction. Our respective *taxi-brousse* trucks arrived, and the Antandroy man left Antananarivo to return south to his homeland. Heading out of Antananarivo toward the east coast, I wondered why I had been warned to beware of this musician (and "his kind"?).

There are eighteen to twenty different groups of Malagasy people that are usually recognized in Madagascar. Merina are predominant in the central Haut Plateau region, which includes Antananarivo. The man at the *taxi-brousse* station who had warned me about Antandroy was Merina. In the Tamatave region on the east coast, the most populous group is called Betsimisaraka. This name means literally "the many who don't separate," though Betsimisaraka are also recognized in Madagascar as comprising two distinct groups, Northern and Southern Betsimisaraka, each reportedly distinct from the other in temperament, custom, even language. Among some of the other, varied groups in Madagascar, Antandroy (from the south) in particular are sometimes construed to be fierce and contentious in temperament, even to be murderous "savages," as people to be shunned and avoided at any cost. In my yet limited Malagasy, I asked the others on the *taxi-brousse*, mostly Betsimisaraka and a few Merina, if there were any Antandroy in Tamatave. Echoing the earlier admonition, an elder Malagasy man responded, "Iah, misy maro izany. Fa tandremo!" (Yes, there are many. But beware of them!)

Numerous Merina have resettled in Tamatave, attracted commonly by the business opportunities there. Indeed, some of the largest commercial enterprises in Tamatave are owned and run by Merina residents. Antandroy have often come to Tamatave to search for wage labor, which is scarce in their more remote southern homeland. Many Antandroy actually end up being employed by Merina bosses, as night guardians for their businesses. I began to hear more specific tales of Antandroy terror in Tamatave, often told by Merina residents. Stories about Antandroy were always extreme, almost panicked: "Antandroy are fiercely argumentative, confrontational, violent"; "an Antandroy will kill you just to get 1000 Malagasy francs (the equivalent of about 25 cents) from you"; "don't ever go into an Antandroy *quartier*—Antandroy will cut off the head of a stranger who goes foolishly onto their turf."

And then gendered dehumanizing slurs: "Antandroy women don't cleanse themselves"; "they are rough, even violent sexual partners"; "they like to bite"; "they carry disease." With some frequency, other Malagasy thus would describe Antandroy as sub- or pre-human "primitives" who are driven by aggressive instinct rather than by reason.

Antandroy are recognized throughout Madagascar, often apprehensively, as staunch adherents to their ancestral customs, and they are often characterized by other Malagasy by their strongly felt connections to Antandroy ancestral land in the south. There is a history of tenacious Antandroy resistance against French colonial occupation of their southern homeland. Often a harsh, drought-stricken region, this area was one parcel of Madagascar that French colonials were unable to subdue. Antandroy reportedly repelled French rifles with just their silver-tipped spears and their maniacal desire to protect their ancestors' land. Yet somehow this valorous past had ceded to, or devolved into, consistently disparaging tales of Antandroy terror.

* * *

In Tamatave there are Antandroy encampments throughout the market, or *bazary be*. In particular I noticed two large such encampments on the main road which formed one perimeter of the market. Whole families, ranging from the elderly to infants, all live in these two roadside encampments, barely shielded from the nearly constant passing of trucks, autos, and small motorcycles. These Antandroy shelters are pieced together from fragments of sheet plastic, cardboard, and corrugated sheet metal, all tented between deteriorated colonial-style cement buildings and the sidewalk below. In the daytime Antandroy sell fruit, cigarettes, peanuts, and bread from makeshift stands in their places on the side of this busy road. Throughout the evening, Antandroy men are employed by Indian merchants, whose shops provide the only vertical walls of the Antandroy encampments. These Indian shopowners are often called *karana* in Malagasy— a term, likely derived from the word, "Koran," which sometimes carries a derogatory inflection. Antandroy are paid, only minimally, to sit from sundown to sunrise as guardians of these Indian shops. Since Antandroy evoke such apprehension, even terror—they are also said to kill unrestrainedly anyone who steals from them—Antandroy presence itself is enough to deter most any notion of thievery. In my early days in Tamatave, I often noticed Antandroy men, barefoot and clothed in garments soiled and torn from this constant street existence, sitting calmly on the ground in their encampments, contemplative, silver-tipped spears poised against their bodies. They sat straight-backed and intent, gazing out into the Tamatave streets, projecting an aura of personal and collective dignity as well as of loyalty to their *karana* bosses. These Antandroy guardians were seemingly disinterested in my presence, however—they certainly were not about to kill me over pocket change (or what I considered pocket change, yet 1000 Malagasy francs might buy enough rice to make a meal for two or three people).

It can be the rainy season most any time of year in Tamatave. A fond saying among Malagasy is that Tamatave has two seasons: the rainy season, and the season in which it rains. The humidity is often so thick here that stainless steel will oxidize into rust, and a dense fuzzy blue-green patina will grow overnight on leather. Yet Malagasy don't complain about the rain—indeed rain is often a sign with which ancestral spirits, or *razana,* express their pleasure or goodwill to the living. One afternoon during a sunny break in the weather, I was walking past one of the Antandroy encampments on Tamatave's main thoroughfare. From the camp arose the sound of an accordion, played so rapidly, with such intensity and gripping beauty, that I was frozen in place. This was music so complex, so inspired, that it was actually disturbing to hear, as though being cut through or stripped bare with sound. This seemed more than could humanly be culled from a relatively small button accordion, a performance virtually not possible.

The accordionist stopped playing to tend to some Malagasy customers who had approached to buy bananas. At that time I could speak no Antandroy, which linguistically is quite distinct, for instance, from the Betsimisaraka spoken more frequently on the east coast. I felt an urgency to communicate something, unsure of exactly what, to this Antandroy man. At least some expression of heightened musical appreciation. At this moment a teenage Merina boy I had befriended a few days earlier and who spoke both French and Malagasy auspiciously appeared. I experienced "coincidences" such as this quite regularly in Madagascar; Malagasy friends later explained such occurrences to be indications of ancestral spirit approval and assistance, for I was there after all to learn about *tromba*, a Malagasy ancestral spirit possession practice.

This boy, Thierry, was from Antananarivo and was on vacation in Tamatave visiting an aunt. He had seemed delighted to find a *vazaha* friend with whom to spend time and to practice speaking French. He cheerfully agreed to speak to the Antandroy musician for me. I asked Thierry to inquire only if the Antandroy man would resume playing his accordion. Thierry seemed nervous, though, upon actually approaching the Antandroy encampment. He also seemed to have difficulty communicating with the Antandroy accordionist. Thierry turned to me and told me in French that the accordionist, whose name was Magnampy Soa, simply asked if I had a *magnéto*, a tape recorder, and instructed that I return with it the next day at this same time. Later that evening, overwhelmed with excitement—I'd not only be able to listen again to Magnampy Soa, but I'd also be allowed to record his performance—I recalled the Antandroy man at the Antananarivo *taxi-brousse* station, with his radio–cassette stringed instrument. Again, a tape-recording device or its image was being designated by an Antandroy as a significant medium in or for musical production. Specifically, Magnampy Soa was clearly concerned in part with the preservation of his show for me the next day.

By morning the rain had resumed, quite heavily. Research grants had afforded me the latest not only in field sound-recording components, but also outdoor camping equipment, so transporting my electrical devices in the rain posed no threat to their well-being. I again recalled the Antandroy man in Antananarivo, seemingly unconcerned that the rain was dampening his intricately carved stringed instrument. I felt foolish, excessive, remorseful. Why should my equipment, devices only of replication, be spared from the elements, while Malagasy musical instruments themselves, on which such exquisite sounds are created, must face rapid deterioration? Indeed, Magnampy Soa's accordion was caked with street dirt and age, its cardboard bellows frayed in spots, its once white buttons yellow-gray and worn. Accordions and materials with which to build other instruments are difficult, and in many cases impossible, to obtain in Madagascar. Another among many irreconcilable inequities, amidst these masterful Antandroy musicians and instrument builders, it was only my strange, distant possessions which were privileged to protection from the humidity, heat, dust, and wind. An agonizing (and likely realistic) image has continued to haunt me, in which I return to Madagascar in the near future to find that Magnampy Soa and others no longer even have instruments on which to perform. Yet *I'll* still have my collection of well-protected tapes, documenting what once was. Perhaps by instructing me to bring my tape recorder, Magnampy Soa was expressing his own vision of loss, similar to mine. And how could I even begin to give back to Malagasy people, who, among other things, were essentially building an academic future for me?

Upon my arrival at his encampment, Magnampy Soa had his children construct a small corner vestibule out of plastic sheets to keep out the wind and rain during our session—this small hemmed-in space would be our recording studio. I became very fond in particular of Magnampy Soa's children, taking two or even three of them at a time for rides on my one-speed bicycle up and down the streets of Tamatave, to the cheers of onlookers who weren't accustomed to seeing *vazaha* spend fun time with Malagasy. Or accompanying the children to the bakery across the street for sweets, and then taking long walks on the Indian Ocean beach (which was only two blocks away), giggling and splashing together in the surf while speaking in Antandroy.

In the cramped corner space I began to set up my recording equipment, which included microphone stands, numerous

wires, microphone preamps, the recorder itself, headphones—
an excess of machines and connections, especially in contrast to
the *magnéto* more familiar to Antandroy, a small portable self-
contained device. Magnampy Soa sat back watching me set up,
with perhaps a glint of pleasure over my entanglement of things
in this tiny space. He brought his accordion and sat down next
to me, his body up against mine. A few awkward moments—
possibly for us both—passed. Magnampy Soa said nothing to
me, and I ventured only "Misaotra" (Thank you). He took a
small bottle of clear liquid, poured some into a glass, and then,
while speaking heatedly and rapidly, apparently to no one in particular, he poured the fluid (rum) on the ground in the corner
of our recording studio. He was giving a *tsodrano,* a verbalized
benediction and offering to his *razana,* his ancestral spirits. So
musical performance even in this apparently secular setting was
still connected in some way to sacred ancestral spirits. Magnampy
Soa continued his rapid recitation for several minutes, then
poured himself a drink of rum, and then one for me. Everyone—
including his wife, his numerous children, and several neighbors
who had come for the session—laughed and applauded when I
drank (the rum was extremely strong—I'm certain I winced). I
believe I had just honored Antandroy ancestral spirits. Magnampy Soa still had not spoken to me—of course, we had no language in common. He simply pointed to the tape recorder and
made a circular motion with his hand. The wind and rain became
still as he drew the first sounds from his accordion.

Again Magnampy Soa played with incredible intensity, speed,
dexterity, and variation. Sometimes he would coax soft tones from
the instrument, pushing and pulling the bellows slowly and delicately; then he would shift into a forceful playing, overworking
the bellows in a maniacal fervor. Sometimes he twisted the bellows
on his push in and draw out of the accordion, creating a slapping
percussion that seemed to intensify certain rhythmic pulses. He
whistled and hissed sporadically though excitedly as he played,
cigarette dangling from the corner of his mouth, all in sync with
his accordion playing. His powerful body would bounce, jerk,

throb, and slap the pavement, also in time with the accordion. I felt these motions as his body remained in contact with and even pounded against mine in this small space. He would occasionally yell something over his shoulder to the women present. At moments of particularly heightened musical intensity, the women present would fervently begin to clap several different rhythms simultaneously, or to yell out excited, lyrical verbal phrases.

Sometimes Magnampy Soa was smiling while he played, either looking directly into my eyes or with his eyes closed. At other times his face would reshape into an expression of painful heaviness or longing. Magnampy Soa was clearly absorbing into his own body the sounds he produced, yet he reciprocally seemed to be giving up his body to some musical/spiritual experience that was beyond my grasp. He was there with me in this moment, yet not there as well, carried in part by sound toward some recollection, imagination, communion with his ancestral spirits. Magnampy Soa played without pause through both sides of a ninety-minute cassette tape, and with the click of the end of side two, he abruptly brought his performance to a close. Again we were faced with an incommunicative awkwardness. All I could say was "Tsara be izany!" (That was great!) By this time it was only drizzling slightly. Magnampy Soa got up and went about his business with his fruit stand.

I wasn't certain how to compensate Magnampy Soa for this session. Another impasse—most people I knew in Madagascar were in constant need of material essentials. Yet play-for-pay sessions might only mean contrived performance settings. I was apprehensive that such sessions would likely impede the establishment of more personal relationships with Malagasy people— I didn't want to become known as some culture broker who would simply pay to obtain a good video or audio recording. My work also depended upon experiencing things as best I could as they usually occur in Madagascar (my own presence at most ceremonial events of course was quite unusual or unnatural). In Antananarivo stories were told in particular about Japanese film crews who had gravely taken advantage of Malagasy generosity.

I was fond of Malagasy people and felt a loyalty and perhaps even a protectiveness toward them and their practices. So how to help out yet not commodify in the process? (Or was this even possible? Perhaps there really was no way to equitably do what I had come to Tamatave to do.)

I went into the store Magnampy Soa was paid to guard and I bought him a pack of cigarettes and a half-litre of rum. Along with these I gave him a constrained sum of Malagasy francs. I felt extremely close-fisted. That evening I made him a copy of the tape we had made together. When I brought it to him the next day, he seemed surprised by the gift, and said, "Tsisy vola" (There's no money). He must have thought that I wanted him to pay for the tape. Magnampy Soa was unaccustomed to being given things by *vazaha*. Indeed, I later learned that he rarely if ever had any contact at all with them. There was another story I occasionally heard among Merina or Betsimisaraka, a recollection of the practices of earlier Protestant missionaries in Madagascar, who offered gifts to Malagasy as an enticement to convert.

I thereafter regularly visited Magnampy Soa and his family, each time bringing food items—kilos of rice and meat, sometimes fish, beans, or cheese—or medications if anyone was ill. I refrained from giving cash on each visit or later for the *tromba* ceremonies I would attend with Magnampy Soa (except for the customary offering of perhaps rum and some coins to the ancestral spirits). He seemed content with this arrangement. He never asked me for money, nor for much else. In fact, once it was clear to him that I would be a long-term resident in Tamatave, that I truly liked him and his family, that I would continually be coming back just to visit, to eat rice on the ground with him, to play music with him, Magnampy Soa even told me not to bring food each time, that it was Antandroy custom to feed a guest, not the other way around. He only asked that someday when I would no longer need it, I give him my bicycle.

I was establishing strong connections with other Antandroy in Tamatave as well. I spent long hours playing *valiha*, another Malagasy stringed instrument, with Velontsoa, a brilliant and imaginative musician. Velontsoa's determination in building his instruments, in showing me how to play them, in performing many straight hours in cramped *tromba* houses, was unflagging. His wife, Mendoe, would sit through the night at a small stand near Magnampy Soa's encampment selling peanuts and cigarettes to *pousse-pousse* (a rickshaw-like vehicle) drivers, prostitutes, and drunken military men. Her young children often fell asleep in my lap as I sat with her chatting throughout the night. In the daytime, with one of her children on each shoulder, we would go gleefully to the market, or I might take the children to the beach so that Mendoe could have a rare moment for herself.

I spent the most time with Vinelo, an Antandroy man about my age. Vinelo and I would take long walks through Tamatave, joking and laughing heartily, stopping to drink some *divay* (wine, from the French *du vin*), and returning to his encampment to play music together and sit all night under the huge Tamatave sky talking as though we were two childhood friends. Vinelo was intent on having me experience with him as much as possible of Antandroy life. He was known to be one of the most powerful younger Antandroy healers in Tamatave, and he would have me sit beside him through numerous ancestral ceremonies. To heal, Vinelo would become possessed by varied royal Malagasy ancestral spirits. It was highly emotional to sit next to my friend as he transformed, often painfully, into revered royal Malagasy personalities from the distant past. Vinelo wouldn't remember the moments during which he was possessed by spirits, so he would always want me to recount for him, and to tell especially what had happened between the spirits and myself. Generally these Antandroy spirits as well were quite kind and welcoming to me.

* * *

Underlying the myth of the Antandroy savage in Madagascar is an acknowledgment among most Malagasy of the exceptional spiritual prowess of Antandroy. Numerous times I was approached by members of other Malagasy groups, who asked to be taken to an Antandroy healer for some sort of assistance, even though there might have been an abundance of healers within their own groups or communities. While most Malagasy believe in one way or another in the *razana,* the collective of ancestral spirits, it seems that too much spirit power in the wrong hands is often feared to be a bad thing, even a manifestation of evil. This sentiment among Merina in particular, many of whom are Protestant, likely reflects a Christian-inspired disdain for any spirit(s) other than the One. Indeed, if Merina were not the ones telling tales of Antandroy terror, it was usually other Christian Malagasy. Among Betsimisaraka in Tamatave, Catholicism tends to be more prevalent than Protestantism; *tromba* spirit possession, however, is also widely practiced among non-Christian Betsimisaraka.

Merina can lead an existence *entre-deux.* They often practice Christianity while at the same time performing ancestral customs such as *famadihana,* in which the bones of ancestors are unearthed and honored as material mediums of departed loved ones. Whereas this *entre-deux* mode of experience can be a cause for anxiety among Merina, Antandroy can exist perhaps more effectively *entre-deux* in a different sense—between the world of the living and the world of the dead—without feeling the inherent obstacles to their beliefs and practices that Christian doctrine imposes. Antandroy bring into the present a past from which some Merina have in ways disconnected themselves—for instance, *tromba* spirit possession itself is often shunned by Merina, especially those more economically privileged. The past with which Antandroy connect so effectively is a past Merina must filter through ever-present reservation (to put it mildly) emanating in part from their experience as Protestants. Among Merina, then, Antandroy are often an ambivalent force. Antandroy evoke fear and apprehension. Yet as their compulsion to tell tales of savagery and terror makes evident, Merina are also fascinated with Antandroy.

And qualities of sound production also play into such an ambivalence. Merina and other Christian Malagasy commonly complain fervently that they find Antandroy music to be distasteful, that it is incomprehensible to them, even demonic. This last evaluation perhaps brings to mind more widespread tales of musical virtuosity so pronounced that it is feared to have been acquired only through making some pact with the devil. Indeed, I've described my own reaction of being even disturbed by the intensity of Magnampy Soa's playing in particular, although this reaction has always seemed primarily an invigorating experience for me, a "disturbance" of what seems humanly possible; yet perhaps voices from my own past impede an unfettered feelingfulness for this extra-human quality. Through their expertise in musical improvisation, in manipulating (what might be thought of as) a somewhat constraining diatonically tuned instrument, in composing and remembering such intricate music, Antandroy are able to create what others often hear as an excess of sound, which then signifies in part a dangerous excess of spirit connection and power.

Magnampy Soa's ancestral spirits would not take human form in *tromba* possession ceremonies unless they were coaxed and appeased with the proper mode of musical performance. It is primarily sound that allows spirit to become embodied. And once spirits do take human form in the present, it is musical performance that often directs their actions and feelings, to which these spirits cede much control. Likewise, the *magnéto*—in its ability to project, reproduce, and indeed symbolically nationalize local practices—itself signifies power among Antandroy, as it represents a heightened sound-dependent capacity not only to please ancestral spirits, but also to enter into contractual rapport with them so as to affect a variety of transformations in the present (healing is such a primary transformative process).

Displaying the *magnéto* or its image also involves incorporation—of a *foreign* mechanical device. Antandroy recognize that their *magnétos* are manufactured *ampitany*, which means unspecifically "out there," or outside of Madagascar. Here Other ways of producing and manipulating sound can be taken and absorbed into Antandroy ancestral practice, thus intensifying Antandroy spirit power. I later learned that processes of incorporation even play a vital role in a Malagasy performative aesthetic. Magnampy Soa told me that the very presence of my foreign recording equipment had been appreciated by his ancestral spirits. So he had not requested the recording session to somehow profit with or from the resulting cassette tape (indeed, he was surprised when I gave him a copy). Rather, Magnampy Soa was creating a powerful foreign and electronic aura becoming to his own revered ancestral spirits. Such incorporated presences inevitably heighten Antandroy (as well as other Malagasy) ceremonial efficacy.

* * *

Some Malagasy were clearly expressing a desire to have a say in constructing a particular ethnographic Self. Christian Merina and Betsimisaraka wanted to influence the path of my (or really their) ethnography, castigating Antandroy *as even more* Other, and placing themselves, in even another sense, somewhere *entre-deux*. In constructing this Antandroy Other in such a derisive light, Christian Malagasy were also trying to construct themselves as *not* Antandroy, as *not* "primitives." Karen Tranberg Hansen in this volume also describes an occasion in which an ethnographic "subject" himself attempts to determine the field of study, indeed to create the (other) Other. And I've often thought about how we construct ourselves, as authors, as authorities, as scholars, as musicians (rarely out of earshot of some mode of World Beat groove) in our own world of difference. Back in the United States, I've since felt another sort of musical disturbance (not at all invigorating) over sound bits and musical nuances so frequently borrowed from our own ampitany, an often faceless and voiceless "out there" in music's big business. "Home" has come as well with numerous other disturbing facets—for instance, its inescapable consumer excess and waste, these in the face of vivid recollections of starvation and environmental devastation which continue to haunt me. As Christian Malagasy had constructed some of their own "field" parameters for me, perhaps Malagasy people and Madagascar itself had also effectively reconstructed me, so well that I would no longer fit comfortably into an often painfully familiar scheme of things back home.

* * *

After nearly two years in Madagascar it was agonizing to prepare to leave. There were strong connections with many Malagasy people—our farewells were emotional, on both ends. Furthermore, I knew that soon I'd virtually never even see or talk with my neighbors, that my friends would be too busy to spend much time socializing, that children would be too well overprotected to ever walk and joke with a stranger. I'd barely even spoken English in the past two years.

Vinelo insisted on accompanying me at six in the morning to the *taxi-brousse* station and on carrying some of my numerous bags. After all the experiences we had together in Madagascar, after all Vinelo had given me, he had asked the day before if I would buy him a four-dollar pair of leather sandals he had his eye on in one of the *karana* shops. On the way to the *taxi-brousse* station, Vinelo said, choking back emotion, "Tsara be andeho hody" (It's good to get to go home). I think he was trying to ease an anxiety we both felt, that it would be a long time before we'd see each other again.

The God of Doorways

KIRIN NARAYAN

"The problem with having two homes, Bahenji," said Mangala as they walked toward her home village, "is that wherever you are, you worry about the other."

"Absolutely," said Charity. She tried to remember Mangala's words in the mountain dialect so that she could later write them in her notebook; they would be a nice addition to the chapter she was trying to revise on women's views of patrilocality and village exogamy as depicted in folksongs.

Mangala's *dupatta* lay around her shoulders. Ever since the bus had left them off where the tarred road ended, she had become a daughter who did not have to veil. Head uncovered, curls escaping from her braid, she had a happy, girlish look.

Skipping at her mother's side, Nabbo sang out in a sweet high voice.

> Lammiyan jammiyan gaajaraa bari lammi khajur
>
> > A long, strong carrot,
> > Very long dates.
> > I climb the balcony to look out:
> > My father's house is so far away.

Mangala clicked her tongue and caught Charity's eye. Deep dimples had appeared in her cheeks. "This girl has no idea what she sings about!" she leaned toward Charity to murmur.

Charity smiled as Nabbo danced along, two braids swinging with pink ribbons at their ends. Charity had immediately recognized this song as one of many contrasting a woman's home of marriage to the home of birth. She remembered how, five years ago, when she had first heard and transcribed this song, Mangala had assured her that the lead line was filled with nonsense words to "make the step." But Mangala's face had sparkled with dimples and mischief, lighting up the erotic referent. At that time, being unmarried and a presumed innocent, Charity had pressed her face into blank and earnest incomprehension.

Mangala continued, "Anyway, Bahenji, now you know how, with marriage, your heart is broken in two. One part is forever in your *piyokhiaan,* your parents' home. But then the attachment to the other home also grows. When you actually can visit your parents' home, like we're doing now, your mind won't leave the other place and all its responsibilities. Has the cow been milked properly? Has your man been fed? Are all the children going to school?"

"Daddy isn't even there!" said Nabbo, giving her mother a push. "He's been teaching near Shimla for at least two years. And it's only Buntoo going to school today. You're like a film actress, making up this sad story."

"*Chup!* Listen to this girl! Too smart for her own good. Just wait till we send you off to your in-laws' and let's see if you speak to your mother-in-law like that. I'm trying to tell Bahenji about what every woman feels, I'm not talking only about my own feelings."

"Bahenji, do you feel this way?" Nabbo asked.

"No shame! Are you writing a book about Bahenji or is Bahenji writing a book about us? Go on, give her an interview."

"Bahenji, in America do you have the *maape* and the *saure,* the home of parents and the home of the in-laws?"

Charity didn't know how to respond. How could she even begin to describe the ways she felt inwardly split and never in the right place? She adopted Mangala's tone of generalization and said, "In America people keep moving all the time, so there usually isn't just one home to leave or one home to go to. This is the same for both men and women."

"What a fate!" Mangala shook her head. "The more homes, the more your heart is broken into little pieces."

Nabbo seemed satisfied. She skipped ahead, singing the catchy tune.

> A long, strong carrot,
> Very long dates. . . .

* * *

Charity had visited this village once before, when she was doing her dissertation research. In those days, you had to walk two kilometers beyond the end of the bus line. The place had shimmered with Mangala's nostalgia, making the trip magical for Charity too. They had arrived at the end of the rainy season, just before the ritual of Hariyali, and for reasons that Charity could no longer recall, the entire village had been squatting or standing outdoors in the dusk, awaiting a glimpse of the first star. Charity had felt she was visiting the edge of the world, a place where the present slipped into the gentle horizon of a safe, enclosed past.

Only a few years had passed, but now the bus came almost to the village's mouth. The *kapoc* trees still grew tall and magnificent, framing views to the snow peaks, and the wheat in the fields rustled gold. Yet amid all these visual rhapsodies, Charity could not entirely screen out the gray uniformity of urban India that had started to creep over this village too, pulling it back over the edge of imagined spaces. Cement had been poured over the smooth old river stones of the cobbled path. A man was wheeling a scooter ahead of them. A cluster of square concrete houses that Charity did not remember had grown up in the fields, one with a satellite dish like an umbrella resting atop it. A tangle of faded and frayed plastic bags lay at the edge of the road. Thinking of urban India immediately sent Charity's mind swooping down to Nick: how was he making his way in that polluted world of the plains, jostling with people and traffic on his trip to visit his mother's relatives? She thought again of the sweetness of joking back and forth about the Indian-English on the invitation to the very wedding that she and Mangala were now going to attend the preliminary ceremonies for. "Marriages are settled in the Heaven and solemnized on the Earth," she had read aloud from the card. "RSVP, Nears and Dears," he had responded, slapping his tongue against his palate so that he sounded like some version of an Indian-Indian instead of an Indian-American.

Whenever she remembered Nick, she had to work on keeping a smile from her face. It was crazy, crazy, absolutely mad. When she thought of being close to him, she imagined a perfect understanding: someone who intuited her mind and each move of her body. Someone to whom she would never have to explain herself, she was so fully accepted and admired.

And yet, for him to really know her would be to undo the glamorous scholar whose dissertation he had read, the scholar to whom he, the humble graduate student, wrote letters laden with obeisances. She might have felt like less of a fraud if, on her arrival, she had brought herself to confess her unemployment to him. But it had hurt her heart too much to think about not having a job anymore, and her throat always seemed too sore to formulate the words. To tell him that she had descended from being a visiting assistant professor to picking up courses as an adjunct professor, to having no job at all, and all this in order to stay home, beside her tenured husband, Isaac—the story seemed too pathetic to begin.

* * *

"It's Kaddu!" called Mangala's mother, lumbering down the front steps to embrace her grown daughter, calling out a nickname that no one in Mangala's house of marriage used. The two women hugged. Then Mangala's mother enveloped Nabbo, too. She put an arm around Charity's back for a quick moment, switching to Hindi to say, "Come, Bahenji, come."

Mangala's tall, angular sister-in-law, Bimlesh, stood by the doorway, looking bemused. When the excitement had lessened a little, she embarked on her own embraces. The visitors were all led indoors into a new cement addition where a sofa set was neatly arrayed. Bimlesh turned on the light, looking expectantly at them.

"So it's all finished now, how lovely," said Mangala, rapturously looking around at the sofas and at the plastic laminated posters on the wall. Charity recognized the Eiffel Tower. Another poster was of two fluffy orange kittens staring at a goldfish in a wineglass. LOVE NEVER ENDS, declared an inscription beneath it. A vase with plastic flowers balanced on a shelf. A white crocheted cover veiled the television. The sofas were maroon and had the slightly unfinished look of work by a village carpenter making objects new to him.

"Beautiful, beautiful," said Mangala in an awed undertone. "How beautiful. It looks like what you'd see on the television. I keep telling Nabbo's father to build us something like this. But does he listen? No!"

"Sit, sit," said Bimlesh. "I'll make you tea."

"This is how it is, Bahenji," said Mangala, dimpling at Charity. "Tea is being brought to me! When you come back, you're a guest in your own home."

Bimlesh went off, and Mangala's mother sat cross-legged in one of the chairs, beaming at her daughter, drinking her presence in. The mother was a rotund woman with a hooked nose and hair that was only gray around the temples. The last time they had visited, the mother had not been home. Charity calculated that if Mangala was in her thirties, then, given the fast turnover of female generations in Trigarta, Mangala's mother could be as young as her early fifties. Having a daughter-in-law, and being a widow, though, gave Mangala's mother the authority of a white-haired generation. Among upper-caste women who were allotted just one man for life, being widowed was final.

"So, she's married now?" Mangala's mother asked, indicating Charity with her chin.

"Oh yes!" said Mangala. "A po-fessor. He has his own car."

"A car," Mangala's mother nodded. "*Khara, khara:* that's right, that's good. Has he come with her?"

"No. He's there in Umm-reeka."

Mangala's mother lowered her voice, turning her head from Charity, but Charity could catch the murmured words. "No children?"

Mangala called out to Charity. "Look, Bahenji, even my mother is asking why you don't have any children. Just like I said, where's my nephew? She's asking for her grandson!"

Charity pressed her lips in what she hoped was a suitably friendly and enigmatic smile that would declare this topic to be painless but closed.

Mangala's mother regarded Charity, looking over her short blond hair, her handloom *salwar-khameez*, the married woman's *bindi* at the center of her forehead. "Does she understand what a *gidda* is?" Mangala's mother asked.

"I understand," said Charity. She was getting tired of being treated like a deaf-mute who needed an interpreter.

"Of course she understands, what do you think? How many times I've told her how you dress up for a *gidda*, Amma, how you and Bimlesh dance together. I've been promising and promising her: if there's a good wedding in my home village, then we'll go for the *gidda*. Why else would we come all this distance just for one night?"

"*Miyo!* One night! All this way for one night? Things were better before these buses. At least then, when people visited, after walking so far they would stay awhile. None of this 'one night,' Kaddu. You'll stay here for a week."

"No, Amma, I can't do that. With Nabbo's father gone, and with Bibi's knees giving her trouble, and the children's school, it's impossible for me to go away now. And the cow, she's really willful. She only lets me milk her. Everyone else gets her kicks." Mangala smiled. She was very proud of her cow. "You should see how much milk she gives! In our house these days there's no shortage of curds and *ghee*."

"Milk, curds, and *ghee*!" Mangala's mother cried. "Then how did you get so weak?"

Mangala laughed. Charity knew well from her own experience that to be accused of being weak and thin was a way of being shown affection. "Look, Bahenji," Mangala said. "Ever since I married, she thinks I'm looking weak. It's only because she doesn't believe that anyone else can feed me like she did."

"Let Bahenji see for herself what a healthy girl you were when you ate your father's food." Mangala's mother waved at a photograph on the table. She reached over, picked it up, and presented it to Charity, speaking with slow vehemence. "This was Kaddu! Was she healthy or not? This is how she looked when we sent her to her in-laws!"

"She was healthy," said Charity, looking at the studio picture in which a plump-cheeked, unsmiling, adolescent Mangala stared out bleakly. "What a round face. I can see why you called her Kaddu. Did she cry when you ate *kaddu*?"

Kaddu meant "pumpkin"—a perfect nickname for little girls with round cheeks. In most households where there was a Kaddu there was also a story about how the small Kaddu had been terrified in the monsoon season when pumpkins grew on vines, when someone suggested that *kaddu* be "cut" for supper.

"Oh, she understands everything!" cried Mangala's mother, staring at Charity in wonder. "She even speaks such *spasht Angrezi bhaasha,* such clear English, that I can understand it too!" Mangala just laughed and Charity did not want to curdle the flow of good feeling she had generated by asserting that she hadn't been speaking English. This was not the first time that someone, hearing mountain dialect from her English-speaking lips, had assumed that it was English emerging in an exceptionally comprehensible manner.

* * *

After tea and lunch and tea again, they set off through the narrow lanes of the village. Along the way, people stopped and greeted Mangala, always calling her Kaddu. Many indicated

Charity, inquiring who this stranger could be: "Sai kun?" they asked. "Sai kun?"

The sounds of a band and general chaos led them through the pine gateway marked WELL-COME. A brass band was playing a jazzed-up version of the popular devotional song, "Om Jai Jagadish Hare." The men wore red uniforms fraying around the wrists. Inside the courtyard, the sound of women singing grew louder. Charity followed the others into a smoky room.

A young man who for this day and for days after would be known only as "Laada," or "Groom," squatted on a low wooden seat, wrapped in a black blanket beside a ceremonial fire. The oil ceremony was under way. Women lined up, one by one, to slip money into a leaf cup and then pour oil within a wreath of straw woven with red cloth, which balanced on the groom's head. Along the edges of the walls, women were crowded together, seated on cotton rugs. As Mangala entered the room, various women got up to enclose her in slow, swaying embraces: one cheek, another cheek, the first cheek again. Everyone stared at Charity with open curiosity. Then space was made for them to sit down.

"Do they have weddings like this in America?" a jolly woman wanted to know, once Mangala had caught up with the news.

"The weddings are different," said Charity.

"I heard that they wear white, poor things, that they don't know white is for widows," declared the woman whose knee was digging into Charity's back.

"It's all customs," Mangala loftily said. "Customs are different here and there. We have a photo of our Bahenji on her wedding day. No red, no gold nose ring, no crown for the groom, poor fellow. If you didn't know the customs, you'd have no idea these people had gotten married!"

Charity remembered the picture. For years it had adorned their refrigerator door, a couple frozen in their own happy moment as life went tumbling onward. "People in America think that red is a shameless color," she said.

"*Ala?*" the women clucked.

The groom was led outdoors for a bath, clipping along in wedding clogs with red satin bands. As he passed, he looked curiously at Charity, and Charity looked down with a demure half-smile. Like most grooms in this area, he was in his mid-twenties. He looked very tired, with large sad eyes. For a moment, she thought he had looked like Nick. Then she told herself not to see Nick everywhere.

Charity drifted out to the courtyard with Mangala and a few others, as the groom squatted on a low wooden stand and a bucket was set beside him. Through the crush of bright women's clothes, Charity could see the graceful strength in the young man's upper arms, the hair on his chest, the glinting water on his brown skin. She did not want to think about men's bodies right now. "I'm going to tape inside," she said to Mangala, who nodded, mouthing the words of the ritual song for bathing.

Back indoors, Charity took her recorder and her notebook out of her case. She recognized the song the women were now singing, about a passing soldier who flirts with a woman by the well. As the tape recorder turned, she composed herself by writing, taking her time to choose each word.

Women cluster close on cotton rugs. They are dressed up in shiny fabrics. In the room there is the starchy smell of new cloth, the sweetness of burning *dhoop*. When the anthropologist pulls out her notebook, dozens of eyes converge. The band must be taking a break, for now there are only these songs. Light filtering in from the door and windows softly illumines the planes and angles of women's faces. Some women sing actively, others mouth words. Between songs, there is the soft burble of conversations, the tinkle of glass bangles like a swift trickle of icy water in the heat. Now and then, a child's cry cuts through the hypnotic joining together of voices.

She reveled in the sense of heightened sensitivity that came with trying to write fieldnotes, along with a conviction of the importance of this experience. Too much of her life slid by, barely noticed.

The biggest gift in observing other people, Charity thought, was that an anthropologist was forced out of her own skin. It seemed like the first time in weeks that Charity didn't have Nick running through her brain in a parallel reality. But as soon as she recognized this, there he was again, with his oversized hands and his glowing brown eyes.

* * *

The groom was dressed up in a suit, with black kohl rimming his eyes. A garland of rupee notes was placed around his shoulders. The groom's crown—the *sahera*—was bound on his head, the long tinsel fringe hiding his face. The other men wound sharp pink turbans around their heads.

In the courtyard, the groom took one last sip of his mother's milk. Though a gauzy *dupatta* was thrown over him and his mother for this intimate moment, and he brought his head near her sunken chest, he actually drank milk from a steel glass she offered. Then he mounted a horse to take him down to the main road, where a bus and taxis waited.

Dozens of posters declaring "Ajay weds Kamlesh" were pasted along the sides of the bus. Women sang as they followed the groom, as the sea of pink turbans disappeared into the bus, and as all the vehicles set off in a cloud of dust. Then they stopped singing, and broke off into smaller groups to chatter as they made their way back to the village. It was late afternoon, with pouring sunshine. A few small clouds floated above the mountains.

"Now we can go prepare for the *gidda*!" said Mangala with the giddy excitement Charity remembered from other times when all of the men in a settlement had departed, leaving the women alone.

"When the men go we can say whatever comes to our lips," said Mangala's sister-in-law, Bimlesh. She giggled, turning to one of the women walking in the group with them. "Oh Asha, tell us that joke."

"Oh yes," Asha said. She was the woman who had wanted to know about American wedding customs. She was a plump woman wearing a shiny fuchsia polyester outfit, with lots of red lipstick and red *sindoor* in the parting of her hair. "I heard this when I was at the wedding in Tikkar. See, there was a dumb boy there, he's so handsome and he's even in government service at a bank. But he can't speak. A woman there said, 'So what if he can't speak? His bulb is the same,' and she told us this joke about a bulb. An old woman went to an old man and asked him for cotton. He felt between his legs and said, 'I don't have cotton, mother. But I have a bulb.' "

Everyone but Charity laughed uproariously. What was the joke? She didn't get it. Maybe something to do with old cotton garments being used as menstrual pads? Or light bulbs, with their shape of swollen balls, being screwed into sockets in order to beam brightness? Or that old people being sexual was always hilariously absurd? She would have liked to ask Mangala, but another woman in the group was already speaking.

"Near where I live there's a shopkeeper who likes to display eggplants," the woman declared.

The others were already giggling in anticipation.

"One long eggplant, two short round ones, that's how he hangs them up in front of the shop. None of us women in the village could walk by that shop without laughing. We had to hide our faces in our veils!"

"When I went to the doctor recently, I almost died with embarrassment," Bimlesh put in. "We were all sitting waiting together and the doctor came out. He asked a woman to raise her *khameez* so he could hear her heartbeat or breathing. Do you know what she did? She took off the entire thing. And there were even men there! When he wanted to give her an injection, I thought, what sort of injection is it that he's hoping to poke into her?"

"Oh you're very naughty, very naughty," women said, wiping their eyes with laughter.

It seemed like everyone was shouting and laughing except for Charity. Maybe it was just the need for tea again, but Charity suddenly felt very tired. Her shoulders ached with the weight of her camera, tape recorder, notebook, and water bottle with the filtered water. She thought of how Isaac knew exactly how to press his thumb in the painful spot above her shoulder blade, how he wrapped her from behind. She thought of her own warm kitchen, with Isaac listening to Bach and straining soup, and how, even when her professional life was buffeted, that kitchen had always seemed to hold certainties.

* * *

Dinner was to be another feast with fried, yeasted round *baturu* breads. In the meantime, Mangala's mother and sister-in-law readied themselves for their performances. As Charity, Mangala, Nabbo, a woman with buckteeth, and a woman with spectacles all sat together in the kitchen drinking tea, Mangala's mother bustled about, in and out of the room. She had a naughty smile on her round face and she was singing under her breath. "Naani aai saiyon asaan nahin dasni."

Charity was being put through the usual paces of why her husband wasn't with her, and why she didn't have children. She was used to not being introduced to other women, particularly if they were senior relatives of the people she was with. It would have been taboo for junior relatives to speak the names of their elders. But it was still odd, she felt, to sit answering personal questions issued by women whom she could identify only by the shorthand of Buckteeth and Glasses.

"Here comes Grandma!" called Nabbo, standing by the door.

Mangala's mother entered with a flourish. She had a shawl thrown over her head and was wearing a long skirt of the sort that was once worn by women all the time, but was now only brought out for ritual occasions. She carried a sack over her shoulder. "Anyone for *proiaan,* sweet breads?" she called in a quavering voice. Reaching into her sack, she offered Charity a dung cake. Then she twirled around, and pointed out to everyone that the slit around the drawstring of the skirt opened just by the crotch, revealing the *salvaar* beneath. "Oh dear, oh dear.

Have another sweet cake. This opening here makes it easier for me to pee."

"And do other things!" called out Buckteeth, shouting with laughter.

Bimlesh appeared next, wearing what Charity assumed must be her husband's pants and woolen jacket, with a colorful Kulu cap balanced over her bun. She wore sunglasses. Her face was heavily powdered, with a twirling moustache drawn on. She flourished a walking stick. "Goods, scented goods!" she cried, cocking the walking stick under one arm so both hands were free to flap from inside her trouser pockets. "Want a bite?" She came over to her mother-in-law and made a pretense of kissing her. Then she was amorous with Glasses.

They all set off through the dark toward the groom's house, where the *gidda* was to take place. About twenty or thirty other women had already gathered, this time singing with a drum. Mangala's mother and sister-in-law waited by the gate of pine needles put up for the special occasion. Mangala, Charity, and the others went ahead. A girl with a blue ribbon in her hair was dancing suggestively in the film style as others clapped. The groom's mother rested against the wall, visibly exhausted. When the song was over, Mangala mournfully spoke across the room to the groom's mother that her own mother and sister-in-law couldn't come, that her mother wasn't feeling well.

"What's wrong?"

"How come?"

"And all the men are gone. Should we call a doctor?"

Just then, the two burst in, unleashing a storm of laughs. Mangala's mother went about, hunched over. She took things out of her sack to offer around. In addition to dung cakes, she had crackling bits of plastic, old clothes, bits of a discarded box. "Take your presents from Grandma, Nani," she said, patting other old women on the head as she ceremonially thrust junk in their hands.

Bimlesh was announcing herself as Grandpa, Nanu. She twirled around, saying she was standing upright, and flapped her hands in her pants some more. Others joined in to sing as Charity set up her tape recorder.

Naani aai saiyo asaan nahin dasni.

Grandma's here, girlfriends, we haven't seen much of her.
During the day she shows herself less,
At night she shows herself more.
During the day, she walks like this,
At night she walks like this.

During the day, Grandma hunched like a woman bent over with age and osteoporosis. For the night, she stood up tall and smiling, arm-in-arm with her husband. "Down then up, down then up, do you understand?" Mangala whispered through her giggles into Charity's ear. Mangala's mother and sister-in-law pranced about, bending and extending, for several bouts of the song.

Next, Asha of the smeared red lipstick stood up and took center-stage in the crowded room. She sang in a loud, declamatory voice:

Come along, all of you,
Come along with me.
At Kishan Singh's temple
We'll bend in worship.

The groom's sister-in-law will come,
His mother will come too.
At Kishan Singh's temple
We'll bend in worship.

Switching from song to spoken words, she ordered, "All of you fall down full-length, women!"

"What did you say is full-length?" asked Glasses, bursting with laughter.

"You have to ask me 'What?'" instructed Asha.

"What?" came an enthusiastic response. A few women fell prone to the ground, helplessly shaking with laughter. Asha repeated, "All of you fall down full-length, women!"

> At Kishan Singh's temple
> We'll bend over to worship.

"I'm lifting, women!"

"What?"

An explosion of horrified laughter greeted this statement as the double meanings sank in.

"The flag of Kishan Singh's temple."

"I'm banging, women!"

"What?"

"The band at Kishan Singh's temple."

Someone began to bang a metal plate amid the laughter.

"I'm dripping, women!"

"What?"

"I'm dripping, women!"

"What?"

"Holy water from Kishan Singh's temple."

Loud sounds of retching rose from the back of the room.

"I'm drying up, women!"

"What?"

"The food offered from Kishan Singh's temple."

All of a sudden, someone noticed Charity's notebook and tape recorder. There was outraged hilarity all around. "She's taping all this! Writing it down! Poor thing. She doesn't understand anything. Why is she taping it?" More laughter. One woman fell on top of her friend, braying hysterically, over what Charity assumed was the image of the anthropologist sitting, so diligent and composed, notebook in hand. "And just look where the thing points!" the woman said, grabbing at Charity's microphone to thrust it toward her friend's crotch. Charity reached for the microphone, wondering about the bumps and thumps that would later show up on tape. "Look how she cares for it!" someone called.

"Here's the food from Kishan Singh's temple, women!" Asha tried to regain the center of attention, but someone else had taken a cue from the microphone and had picked up a cricket bat and was making lewd advances at the groom's mother. Buck-teeth got the wooden spoon that had been used to ladle clarified butter into the sacred fire. "*Desi ghee!*" she offered, pointing and poking, while giggling women sitting on the floor shrank away. "Anyone for homemade butterfat?" Asha sat down good naturedly. She had clearly been a success.

An old crone with no teeth and heavy glasses careened around, arms in the air like a scarecrow. At one point she put a plastic basket on her head and sang in a cracked old voice about how Krishna was breaking her water pot. Yet another woman slid her hands under her baggy *salvaar,* flapping and calling out, "I'm itching! I'm itching!" Someone else appeared with a hand-kerchief tied around her head, and a blanket wrapped around her waist. "Here's the Gaddin, the shepherdess," others laughed with delight.

"Ut! Ut! Get up!" Women were being pulled to their feet to dance. Someone tried to grab Charity too.

"Minjo nahin onda—I don't know how," said Charity.

"How long have you been married and you still don't know how?" cried Asha.

By now about half the women in the room were dancing around, singing and shouting. Mostly these were the married women. Nabbo sat with the unmarried girls, conspicuous for their simpler clothes and the absence of red *bindis* and makeup. These girls looked on with faces that seemed awkwardly set. Now and then, they giggled, looking down. Only one of them, the girl with a blue ribbon in her hair, was gyrating about. The old crone slapped her behind. "Go dance in the films!" the old woman cried.

* * *

Charity taped, Charity took notes, Charity stood up with her camera to flash into the chaos. Yet even as she was so busy with immediacies, her mind also had pockets of distance, places where she wandered. She imagined telling Nick about this night, then wondered whether she would be too embarrassed to recount all the goings-on among these "Nears and Dears." She remembered Isaac's disbelief as they lay together under a comforter one winter night and she told him about how women danced the *gidda*. "No way, Charinsky!" he had said, pulling her closer to kiss the top of her head. "Your village women? You'd blow people's minds if you wrote about it."

"I did," Charity had mournfully said, feeling her body draw away from his with the mention of writing. Like the words "job" and "publications," any mention of her writing could sour a moment. "It was in my dissertation. But it's been too long. I have to go back if I want to write something real."

The mention of her desire to go away had in turn made Isaac recoil. Sometimes it seemed that being married was all about being able to map out every step of a possible argument with such precision that there was no need to even open your mouth—you could run it all through in your head instead.

But wasn't this preferable to not having the faintest idea of how someone argued because they viewed you with such respect? Being dazzling with apparent brilliance and success was all very fine if you didn't know that this image was as insubstantial as smoke swirling from a kitchen hearth up into the sunbeams that flooded down through a gap in the slate roof.

* * *

"Narsingh pujna chalo bo chhokariyon!"

Another act was taking over the center stage. Buckteeth and Glasses had emerged with a flat brass *thaali* loaded up with all the implements for worship that had been used earlier in the day: bits of rice, vermilion, turmeric, flowers, a brass bell, an empty brass lamp. They approached Mangala's mother, who began to boom laughter. As they neared, she amiably lifted her skirt and her *kurta,* revealing her ample belly with the baggy *salvaar* tied with a drawstring just below the bulge.

"Come worship Narsingh, girls!" Charity recognized Narsingh as a god of doorways, worshiped each morning at most houses. Also, Narsingh was at the center of a possession cult she had read about in old district gazetteers.

The two women solemnly set down flowers before Mangala's mother's crotch, along with a bit of rice, turmeric, and red vermilion powder. They called for some red thread, which they offered too. "Jai Devadasiya, hail to Devadas!" they muttered with the intonations of a Brahman priest. Devadas was Mangala's dead father's name. "Manni aya? Khel aya?" they asked. "Are you getting possessed? Are you going to let down your hair and whirl in a trance?"

Tears of laughter streamed down Mangala's mother's face as she obediently flung her torso about like a possessed woman. She extracted a few coins from a pouch inside her undershirt, offering these to her worshippers. Ringing the brass bell, Buckteeth and Glasses moved on to other older women whose doorways had seen many passages.

Charity found herself pulled to her feet.

"I don't know how!" she resisted again.

"Of course you know, just dance!" others cried. "Give us a dance from your country!"

"Sing us an English song!"

"I can't sing."

"Then play something on your *tep recard.*"

All eyes were now on Charity.

"Go on Bahenji, go on. We'll all dance to the English song too!" Mangala coaxed. "It'll be so much fun to be foreign women together."

Charity fumbled in her bag, knowing that somewhere down there was a tape she allowed herself to listen to for shots of high energy and connection: a collection she had put together of rock and country hits she particularly liked. She unplugged the microphone and slid the tape into her machine, not knowing what hit would come up. She would have liked Mary Chapin Carpenter singing "Passionate Kisses," a song she had listened to very often these last few weeks, but she couldn't remember where it was on the tape. Instead, she drew "Don't Dream It's Over," by the New Zealand group Crowded House. In a split second Charity had to judge that this would do. She rewound to the beginning of the song and turned the volume of her little machine up as high as it would go. She stepped to the center of the room, and tried to follow the hard rhythm of the electric guitar to free her body from the tight control of the modesty codes she had internalized for Trigarta to the wild abandon the women around her had shown.

"There is freedom within, there is freedom without," the song began. "Try to catch the deluge in a paper cup."

Beside her, Mangala stretched out her arms, gracefully circling her hands from the wrists. Mangala's mother swayed, still in apparent trance. Asha was doing the twist, bending her knees close to the floor and pretending to strum a guitar. Others turned and gyrated. Soon, they were all joining in to sing "Hey now, hey now," but it was only Charity who could untangle the words to add "Don't dream it's over" in the chorus.

A Touch of Danger

KAREN TRANBERG HANSEN

When I saw his name I instantly remembered him. A front-page article in one of Zambia's dailies described him as the Deputy Police Chief of Lusaka Province, who led a riot squad against demonstrating students at the University of Zambia (UNZA) in July 1992. Student riots were fairly common on the university campus, occasioned by politics in the country at large, dismissals of professors, and bread-and-butter issues. This particular event was among the more dramatic ones. I had seen the commotion earlier that day when passing the campus area by bus. Students had blocked the main road with huge stones, lit a bonfire in the middle of the road, and chanted solidarity songs. The name of the police officer in charge—I'll call him Commander Mpunga—jumped at me from the newspaper page with a power strong enough to evoke a vivid recollection of that day in August 1981, when he and two men from the Zambia Police Force and the Department of Immigration asked me to account for myself and my work.

* * *

My friends and colleagues who work in other African settings look at me with disbelief when I tell them that Lusaka, Zambia's capital, is one of my favorite cities. To be sure, Lusaka's ramshackle environment is not beautiful in any conventional sense. In fact, most tourists bypass the capital when visiting Victoria Falls or Zambia's rich game parks. And there is nothing grand about the city, which arises abruptly from the surrounding savanna as a dusty and windy place sprawling across a limestone escarpment. The truth is that I love Lusaka, but in a sort of ambiguous way; part of me finds the city exciting, while another part wishes it would offer its residents much better lives than those they so inventively piece together. What I really like about Lusaka is its lively mixture of people and activities and their hint of dramatic dealings. I am intrigued by the city's biography and history, which are always pressing on with new and surprising twists.

Lusaka is never placid, bland, or uneventful. It pulsates with all kinds of activities. Office high-rises line the downtown streets, where a few colonial buildings are still standing. Here is a watch repairman, and over there women with babies on their backs are selling roasted groundnuts. Newspaper vendors on the corners of sidewalks do a busy trade. A blind beggar accompanied by a young child stood for many years on the very same spot just opposite the post office. Open-air markets and street vendors bridge the city's different zones, connecting the flow of people, goods, and ideas between peri-urban residential settlements and municipal and national administrative headquarters and institutions. Wherever I go, I can feel Lusaka's pulse in what is happening around me.

After close to thirty years of coming and going, I have grown exceedingly fond of Lusaka. My love did not develop at first sight but slowly, "bit by bit" as my local friends say in Zambian English. In fact my relationship with Lusaka received a major jolt in 1981 when I had come back to do follow-up research on household dynamics and women's economic activities in a low-income township on the city's outskirts, where I had done fieldwork for my M.A. in anthropology ten years earlier.

Norah, a township resident, has worked with me as my main, though not always sole, assistant, in all of my research in Lusaka. Locally, she was recognized for her leadership role in one of the major churches as well as for her entrepreneurial initiatives. Thirteen years older than I, she has been my chief advisor and confidante—in short, a close friend. I write about her with a deep fondness tinged with sorrow, for she passed away in 2000. Throughout my work in Lusaka she and her extended household have provided an important reference point. Her personal circumstances are a microcosm of Lusaka's diverse population. She was born in South Africa, where she married her husband, one of the many Zambians who went on labor migration to South Africa during the colonial period. They returned to Zambia soon after independence in 1964 and settled with their children in this township when it opened in 1967.

The township consisted of a population of home owners in self-built housing and a growing number of tenants. It had a teeming market, several legal and illegal bars and taverns, churches, and a variety of social groups and associations that catered to the welfare and recreational needs of its heterogeneous population. By Zambian urban standards, the township was not exactly squalid. It comprised a range of occupational groups, including teachers, clerks, and nurses. Still, when compared with the wealth in the more affluent neighborhoods next to it, the township's poverty was striking. By far the majority of the men who were employed were working as semiskilled and manual laborers. Such employment meant low earnings, and many households had limited economic means.

Aside from occasional weekend visits, I have never lived for any extended period of time in this township, although I have often—as in 1981—explored township residence options. I have not pressed too hard the issue of staying there because of what Norah, her family, and friends construe as my needs—such as running cold and hot water, electricity, television, and entertainment, and our mutual concerns for safety, both theirs and mine. As in Zambia's urban areas in general, this township experiences frequent burglaries and armed robberies. A police post was only established in the early 1990s, and public pay phones and cellular phones are even more recent introductions. This is to say that my township fieldwork has been of the commuting kind, involving daytime observations and weekend and holiday visits.

On my return in 1981, I wanted to explore how the overall economic slowdown of the intervening decade had affected already hard-pressed households. I also had my mind set on assessing the feasibility of a new research project.

During the summer months of 1981, Norah and I trudged through the streets of the township, using plot numbers to identify the houses in which we had interviewed residents in 1971. In cases where the original householders had remained, we took note of household composition; inquired into the ages, whereabouts, and activities of all members; and examined in detail what women were doing. During my first fieldwork in 1971, only about one-third of these women contributed to the household economy with incomes they earned in their own right, a few of them as wage workers, but the majority as small-scale traders, mostly within the township itself. But in 1981 almost all of these women were busy with one form of trade or another, working in their own homes, or from yards, streets, or the township's market. For them, "work" meant trade.

* * *

On that Friday in August 1981 when I first met Commander Mpunga, I had as usual biked to the township in the morning from the university district where I lived as a paying guest in the home of an American colleague. There was no regular connection by bus, the mode of transportation that I used otherwise. Reaching the township involved a twenty- to thirty-minute bike ride, first on the main road, then through a squatter settlement next to one of Lusaka's poshest residential areas, and finally up a steep hill past the township's market and on to Norah's house. I rode a shiny metallic grey British folding bicycle. Before traveling to Zambia, friends had advised me that there were very few bikes available for purchase in the local shops. So I brought my own bike with me into the country. Riding it, I certainly was conspicuous, the more so since Europeans—as whites are called in Zambia regardless of nationality—generally drove cars. When I biked up the last hill out of breath and perspiring, township children practicing their English greeted me in their high-pitched voices: "How are you?" My answer, "I am fine," was promptly picked up by little kids with no English, who greeted me with "I am fine" the next time that I passed them on my bike.

That August, Norah and I were close to completing a series of interviews in the township's market. Because many women had shifted their trade from homes and yards to the township's market, we had decided to extend the study to include a survey in the market to explore the different ways in which women and men were involved in market trade and who, in which trades, were making the most money. The market was a busy, noisy, and dusty place. Like most township markets, this one had a series of covered stalls and a much larger open-air section where hundreds of traders sat on rickety chairs or on the ground. Spread in front of them were their wares: fruits, vegetables, snacks, charcoal, cooking oil, soap, and medicinal herbs. Along the market perimeter there were small furniture workshops, tinsmiths, radio and shoe repair shops, tailors, traders of secondhand clothes, hairdressers, and eating places. Such markets are divided into separate sections for different goods. On that morning we were interviewing women in the live chicken section.

While we were scrutinizing the ins and outs of the live chicken trade, a young boy came up and informed us that we "were wanted at home."

Although I did not recognize this particular boy, I didn't consider the request to be out of the ordinary. Adults in Zambia commonly call on neighbors' children to run errands and bring messages. I thought that it was a boy from the street where Norah lived and that visitors might have arrived who wished to see her.

As we walked through the market, I grew wary. A heavy-set man in a suit fell in with us. And outside the market wall was parked a pickup truck with the UNIP logo on it, the country's single political party then, the United National Independence Party. Two men jumped out of the truck and joined our walk to Norah's home. I did not recognize their khaki uniforms. They were both younger and considerably thinner than the man in the suit.

While we were walking, the man in the suit asked whether I was from the United Kingdom and what I was doing. I told him that I was a Dane and an anthropologist teaching at an American university. "I'm following up on a study I carried out in this township ten years ago," I explained. "I reported to the chairman of the UNIP branch in the township when arriving in June, telling him of the purpose of my work; I also brought letters of introduction to the market authorities." I wondered what his questions meant.

Norah lived very close to the market. When we reached her house, we entered and got seated in her small, neatly furnished living room. There was no observation of the extensive hospitality that customarily accompanies visiting practices in Zambia. "I am Commander Mpunga," said the man in the suit, in impeccable English, pulling out his identification card from the Special Branch of the Zambia Police Force.

I knew that this was the investigative arm of the Police Force, and I tried to remain calm. The Special Branch was Zambia's equivalent to the Soviet KGB or the American CIA. Everyone, Zambians and foreigners like myself, knew that the Special Branch both informed on the activities of "aliens" and harassed locals for no apparent reason. Zambians and foreigners alike had been arrested without warrants, and foreign professors from the university had been deported because of allegations of "subversive" political activity. I was more than worried; I was scared.

Taking charge, Commander Mpunga asked, "What are you doing in our country?" and demanded to see my papers. I showed him my University of Zambia photo identification and the "to whom it may concern" letter that I always carried with me, issued at the Institute for African Studies at the university, and I explained the purpose of my study. This discussion went on for a while. Afterward he asked personal questions about my age and marital status, looked at my questionnaires, and inspected my appointment calendar. The Commander's young colleagues complimented my handwriting and admired the backpack in which I carried my notebook, questionnaires, and other necessities to and from the township. One of the young men asked whether I had reported to the Danish Embassy. "I haven't bothered to do that," I explained, "basically because my stay in Zambia is short, barely three months." Questions then followed about how long I had lived in the United States and about my degree, qualifications, and the funding source of my study.

Throughout these interchanges, I remained puzzled about what was going on. The commander may have read the expression on my face. Establishing clear lines of authority, he said, "Karen, we have not picked you up because you are white. But as you know, there are so many difficulties in Zambia, especially in relationship to the countries to the south." "Yes," I answered in my most polite voice, "of course you have every right to ask who I am." I added that if he and his colleagues wanted to see my research permit and passport, they would have to accompany me to the place where I lived. Commander Mpunga then ordered the two young officers to take me home while he took care of other matters. I imagined that he would report back about the nature and outcome of our interchange to the UNIP authorities in the township.

When Commander Mpunga's two colleagues loaded my bicycle onto the UNIP pickup to set off for the university district, I grew apprehensive. Norah looked particularly ill at ease; she clearly did not know what to make of this. Low-income township residents like her were not used to trusting police, and she looked worried. "I will work in the university library this afternoon," I told her, "and return as usual to the township tomorrow morning, that is, Saturday," trying my best to appear calm and composed and not allowing this event to interfere with our research plans.

I rode in the UNIP pickup truck with the two young officers to the university district; we turned left at the crossroad that led to the Institute for African Studies. I explained to the men that we could go there, if they wanted to inspect my official dossier. There they also would be able, I added, to meet people who could tell them more about who I was and the purpose of my study. They told me that all they wanted to see was my passport, and we drove on. Giving directions, I pointed to the turnoff to Lubumbashi road that led into the university district.

"Do you know where Lubumbashi is?" asked one of the younger men.

"It is in Zaire, on the other side of the copper belt," I explained. "It used to be called Elisabethville during the colonial period."

"Have you ever been there?"

"Oh no, everyone knows that there are lots of troubles in the border region."

Inquiring further, one of the young officers asked if I had been to other countries in Africa. I explained that as a young student in 1969, I had done a brief stint of rural field work in Kenya.

When we reached the place where I lived in the university district, only the two children and two dogs of my American colleague and host, Kathleen, were at home. For security reasons, many foreign households in Lusaka have dogs. Such dogs are usually trained to be aggressive toward intruders, especially black Zambians. When we arrived, the dogs started barking. Seeing the dogs, the young officers looked wary.

Once I had sent the dogs and the children into another room, I took the men into the living room and showed them my passport, research permit, United States alien registration card, identification cards from the university and the state of Minnesota, and my American Express card. Credit cards were not widely used in Zambia in those days, and it clearly intrigued them. "It works like money," I said, explaining how we use credit cards in the West. They thumbed through the pages of my passport and wrote down some details. One of them asked if Seattle was in Denmark. I explained that my passport had been issued at the Royal Danish Consulate in Seattle while I was a graduate student at the University of Washington and that my visa to

Zambia and entry and exit stamps from my first visit were in my canceled passport.

I still did not understand why I was being questioned. "How," I asked the men, "am I to explain this sudden interruption of my work to the people in the township?"

One of the men pulled out an identification card from the Immigration Department and explained that the Immigration Department had to see whether my research permit and visa were in order. This sounded plausible. Indeed I had been held up at the immigration desk in the airport when entering the country because I did not bring along copies of chest x-rays. To safeguard against tuberculosis, such photos were requested in the research permit. The request was printed in tiny script, which I had overlooked. Still, I had gone to the x-ray department of the university hospital immediately after arriving, duly reporting with the photos to the downtown immigration office. There, I had received the necessary stamp on my passport. Really, what was all this fuss about?

The men left. This took place on a Friday morning. Little did I know that this encounter was one of several that were yet to take place. In the afternoon my host Kathleen, who had noticed how the morning's events had unsettled me, offered to drive me to the township to talk with Norah. I was glad to relieve any worries she might have had about what had happened to me. I explained to her what I had been told: the incident had been a minor immigration matter.

Later that afternoon I deposited a duplicate set of field notes and my diary at the nearby house of some American friends who were colleagues at the university. I still worried. I took this step to retain a set of notes in case of further police interference in my work. I also recorded the events of that Friday and events that followed in a plain Zambian exercise book that I hid among the children's schoolbooks. Meanwhile, Norah and I continued our work in the township on Saturday and Monday, while I kept wondering what to make of what had happened.

* * *

That weekend, my host Kathleen and her two children flew to Kenya to visit her husband, who was conducting research there. She had arranged for a Zambian friend's two teenage daughters to keep me company while she and the children spent a week in Kenya. Right after sunset on Monday night one of the girls told me that there was a man at the security gate. I went outside and said "Good evening" to the man who was hanging at the gate. He smelled distinctly of beer.

"Don't you recognize me?" he asked. I didn't, at least not at first sight. The man wore civilian clothes. He explained that he was the person who had driven the UNIP pickup truck that had brought me home from the township the previous Friday.

"Oh," I responded, "what is the matter now?" He needed to see my personal papers again.

I said that I wanted to see an identification card and he pulled out his Zambian national registration card, a document that everyone carries. "This isn't enough," I said, after which he produced his Police Force identification card.

Taking the man inside the house, I first sent the dogs into another room. Once he was seated in the living room, I expressed my surprise at his request. "Why is this necessary?" I asked. "I showed all my official documentation and personal papers to you and your colleagues last Friday." When I brought out my papers again, he said that he was going to take them all to police headquarters, including my credit card.

"You need a warrant for this," I argued, putting the papers into my handbag and proceeding to sit on it. And I asked once again: "Why have you come?"

This time he explained that he needed to see my questionnaires. I gave him some empty forms to look at.

"Where have they been printed?"

"At the Institute for African Studies," I explained.

Finally he said that he had to take the questionnaires that had been filled out, that they were going to study them at police headquarters, that I was to report there at 8:30 the next morning, and that I should bring my official and personal papers with me.

When leaving he asked, "Where are the owners of the house?" Not wanting to let him know that my host was out of the country, I lied: "At the university for a meeting with students." I was relieved when he was out of the house and got into the car of a friend with whom he very obviously had been drinking at a nearby university watering hole prior to making the visit.

* * *

Zambia in those days was full of stories of people who had been held in police custody for no apparent reason. In several instances foreign university professors had been declared prohibited immigrants and forced to leave the country. I wanted to call someone, but Kathleen's house, like the majority of university houses then, had no phone. Bewildered and now plain scared, I sent one of the girls to collect my American friends, Susan and Henry, who lived nearby and with whom I had deposited my notes and diary. They in turn contacted a German colleague and friend, Ilse, who worked in an administrative capacity at the Institute for African Studies.

What had caused the Special Branch to seek me out? Why this sudden confiscation of my notes? What was I afraid would happen? Had I been hit on by a drunk African policeman who saw an opportunity to lord it over a young white woman? Because I was frightened to remain alone with the girls in the house, I talked Henry into staying with us overnight. He had lived in Lusaka for several years and was the kind of person who wasn't easily ruffled by surprises.

Over tea in Kathleen's living room my friends and I wondered about what might have prompted this unexpected summons to Police Force headquarters. Informal conversation in this relaxed atmosphere sharpened my recall of potentially relevant circumstances. I described at length my work in the township, the kinds of interactions that Norah and I had had with township residents, and my general sense of what was going on there. My step-by-step recounting in fact revealed a number of issues to which I had not paid much attention.

I told my friends that many people had seen Norah and me walking throughout the township, searching for people, and asking about their whereabouts and activities. We had interacted with people all over the place. To be sure, I explained, our presence had been noted in public, such as in small restaurants and bars where we stopped to drink soft drinks and occasionally beer when we got tired of walking. Had I challenged widespread notions of what was considered to be proper gender behavior in public? Was my daily arrival in the township by bicycle rather than by car unsettling the accepted hierarchy between Europeans and black Zambians? Really, how did township residents see me and define me?

It was also true, I admitted, that Norah and I had socialized a good deal with her "homeboys," the term the township's South African residents used for members of their funeral association, a group that actually organized quite a variety of social activities, usually in the homes of members.

Perhaps more to the point, I told my friends that Norah and I had been stopped on some occasions by church elders and by youth from the township's UNIP organization, who asked us what we were doing. In fact, during the previous week Norah had informed me that one of her church elders had said that it was not a good thing to roam around so widely. Really, had we ventured into territory that was considered to be off-limits?

Because I had reported to the UNIP branch chairman in the township at the outset of my study, I had not taken seriously the offhand remarks and questions that our presence and public behavior in the township evidently were giving rise to. I told my friends that most township residents considered the UNIP chairman to be a rather harmless person who ran his office in the manner of a village headman, and that I simply had assumed that our informal call at his house with my official letter of introduction was sufficient to explain the purpose of my work and presence in the township.

* * *

The next morning, two friends joined me when I reported to the Special Branch at Zambia Police Force headquarters. Ilse had been with me the previous evening when we were trying to figure out the meaning of my meeting with the Special Branch. She is a truly no-nonsense person, always excellent at getting to the heart of things. What is more, she was the research affiliate officer of the Institute for African Studies and married to the Zambian man who then was the university's vice chancellor, the position that corresponds to president in American universities. Ilse carried my official dossier from the Institute. The other friend was Kate, a British colleague who was taking a break in Lusaka from her research in the rural areas of the Northern Province.

At the headquarters of the Zambia Police Force, we reported to the clerk at the reception desk. This was a busy place, with lots of uniformed people coming and going, including the man from immigration whom I had met the previous Friday. "How are you, Karen?" he asked. I was struck by the informality of his greeting. He walked us through some empty corridors and took us into a large office. It was sparsely furnished, containing a couple of tables and ordinary chairs, without curtains or blinds. There were piles of empty envelopes and files on the floor. We seated ourselves and soon after, Commander Mpunga, now in uniform, entered the door. When he had settled himself behind the largest table in the room, he requested our names and addresses.

Ilse interrupted impatiently: "Dr. Tranberg Hansen's background and credentials were scrutinized within the university and by the Immigration Department long before any research permit was issued. What is at stake?" she asked. "What is the problem?"

Commander Mpunga responded authoritatively but patiently that even though such procedures might have been followed, "we can never be certain; people have been known to work undercover even when they have a university affiliation."

After some small talk about who we were, he turned to my research. "How did you select the people you interviewed?"

I explained that my 1971 sample was drawn by house type and that my assistant and I had returned to these same houses to interview householders who had remained in the township over the intervening decade.

Commander Mpunga then informed us that he had requested my notes to check whether I was "searching for people of particular nationalities, regardless of what the official subject of my study was."

"In Lusaka there are people from many places," I responded, "but this township appears to have a majority of people with Eastern Province background."

Turning to my notes, which in fact he had looked over carefully, he argued, "The focus of your study is biased. You ought to study secretaries and women who are in better positions in order to compare. Why," he went on, "do the women in this township not have better jobs?" He was embarrassed, I knew, by the poor circumstances of the women whose lives I was studying.

I explained that I was aware of the limitations of my work, that it would be interesting to study other groups, but that I could only achieve so much during the short duration of my stay in Zambia. "I supplement my own work, trying to learn about the situation of other groups by reading works written by others. When I return to Zambia next time, I hope to extend the scope of my work."

"Why did you not interview the men?"

I explained that many men were away at work during the daytime. "Even though I sometimes visit during weekends, people are busy with visitors and relaxation. I feel that it is an intrusion to interview at such times. And of course the women tell me something about what their husbands are doing."

"Maybe," the Commander retorted, "but Zambia is an egalitarian society, and the focus of your study hides it."

Next he inquired why it seemed as if all researchers at the Institute for African Studies worked in this particular township. "This is not correct," Ilse responded. "They study throughout the country." And Kate said that there were many people like herself who actually lived in the villages while doing research on rural problems.

Commander Mpunga then gave some examples of European men who had married Zambian women and gone to live in the township where I worked. The Special Branch appeared to be well informed about such cohabitational arrangements.

"As far as I know," I said, "I am the only person who has conducted research in that township."

"It would be much better," he continued, "if students from the university would study different aspects of life in Zambia under the guidance of a research director and then put this together into an overall study." Ilse explained that such work indeed was being done under university auspices.

"The goal of the research carried out by people like you," he said, "should be to produce something that would be of use in Zambia."

"I agree with you, but there are two sides to that goal. One is to produce something that is useful in Zambia, and the other is to inform people elsewhere, for instance in the United States, about how people are making a living in contemporary African cities." I added that the results of my 1971–72 study had been quoted and commented on in Zambia, and that I expected that the work that I had just been doing would address how the conditions of poor married urban women might be improved.

"To be sure," he said, "we welcome studies like yours in Zambia."

Surprised by the Commander's swift change of stance, I said that I certainly hoped so, and that I had enjoyed my time in the township, where I had seen considerable progress since 1971. He then commented that Zambia was a developing country and that conditions for women there were different from those in the United Kingdom, for example, where more women were employed. He had seen that himself when he was in England on training. "People there were very cooperative, and Zambians are becoming better at that," he added. "Development," he explained, "takes a lot of time."

We left on a friendly note. Commander Mpunga invited me to report anyone who interfered with the progress of my work in the township directly to him at Police Force headquarters. Even then, I remained puzzled and unsettled by the events of the last few days. How, I asked myself, had my rather innocuous work in the township somehow created the impression that I was a spy or informer? Although Commander Mpunga and his young colleagues had not expressed this in so many words, the allegation was obvious.

* * *

To understand why such a suspicion could arise, you had to walk around Lusaka in 1981 to get an impression of the circumstances that gave rise to economic and political tensions. The capital had a population of about half a million at that time. Half of them lived in squatter settlements. In the late 1960s the Zambian government, professing socialist principles, had nationalized major economic concerns. When world market prices of copper, the country's chief export revenue source, plummeted in the mid-1970s, the economy went on a downslide from which it never recovered. Beginning in the late 1970s, there were several attempts to reform the sluggish economy through loans and aid from the International Monetary Fund, the World Bank, and foreign national governments. But from the point of view of ordinary Zambians, the results of those efforts were by and large disappointing, for they had produced only empty shop shelves in the state stores, scarcities of many goods, and accelerating unemployment. Business activity was much livelier in township markets such as the one in which Commander Mpunga and his colleagues had first found me. Much of what was sold there bypassed the state-controlled marketing system.

These economic woes were accentuated by the country's political involvements. In its antiwhite stance toward the settler regimes in South Africa and Rhodesia, the Zambian government closed export–import routes to the south; supported the work of the Zimbabwe African National Union (ZANU), the liberation movement that led Rhodesia to become Zimbabwe in 1980; and hosted the headquarters of the African National Congress (ANC), in exile from South Africa. The political tensions were high, provoked by the white South African government's sponsoring of counterinsurgency movements in the Zimbabwe liberation war and its spying and informing on ANC activities in Lusaka. Who was a friend or foe in such a setting? And what was this anthropologist from America with a Danish passport who rode a funny-looking bicycle and spoke with a German-sounding accent doing there anyway? To Zambian ears, my accent sounded somewhat like Afrikaans, the language of the detested Boers, the whites of Dutch descent who then held political power in South Africa.

During those years there were several incidents of South African-instigated bombings in the whole frontline region, within Mozambique, Botswana, and Zambia. They included the bombing of a ZANU training camp on the outskirts of Lusaka, not far from the township where I worked. All Lusaka residents had experienced the tensions of those years; all had observed a curfew. Some of them had daily contact with exiled South Africans and Zimbabweans involved in liberation efforts who lived in both high-income and low-income areas. The township where I worked had hosted several Zimbabweans in the 1970s, and in 1981 there were ANC people living throughout the community. This I certainly knew. I had been introduced to several South Africans, not in their political capacity, but in their interaction with the "homeboy" association in which Norah was active. Evidently in the view of some township residents who themselves had South African backgrounds, this was akin to snooping.

Against this backdrop it is probably not in the least surprising that my work was questioned. Contemporary anthropological research in a country like Zambia is carried out in a complex world of politicized nationality/ethnicity rather than in communities of discrete cultures and traditions. Many foreign scholars, including anthropologists, were being questioned in Zambia in those days. My training had prepared me poorly for reckoning with the complicated ramifications of the multiplicity of local opinion.

Before my three encounters with officials from the Special Branch, I had never suspected that the world of politics would touch me directly. Had these events occurred at the beginning of my fieldwork rather than toward the end, I might not have carried through with it. Or might I? Given the overall atmosphere of fear, suspicion, and insecurity in which Zambians and foreigners lived in Lusaka in 1981, I did not feel at ease until I reached the transit lounge in Lusaka's international airport, waiting at the gate for my flight. I feared that the bureaucratic exit procedures in the airport might produce yet another surprise. There were currency control forms to fill out, research permits and departure tax forms to be produced, luggage to be examined, and bodies to be frisked. "What a place," I said to myself, looking out the windows of the transit lounge onto the dusty landscape surrounding the capital. When I finally had fastened the seatbelt in the plane bound for Europe, I was unsure about my dedication to return to the new project I had begun to plan prior to going to Zambia that year.

* * *

I did return. Looking back, I confess that I am a bit surprised by my strong reactions to those events of 1981. They really scared me. But I have continued to return. My curiosity about the unfolding of urban life in Zambia outweighed my hesitations. And each time I return and set out on my research, I am overly meticulous about reporting to the Danish Embassy and informing different levels of authorities about my work and presence, contacting them in advance, making social calls during and at the end of my fieldwork. Throughout my subsequent work in the township during the rest of the 1980s and early 1990s the circumstances that embroiled me in a confrontation with investigative police authority in 1981 have changed, especially since 1991, when Zambia's one-party political system gave way to multiparty rule. In 1992, Commander Mpunga had become Deputy Police Chief of Lusaka Province, the UNIP branch chairman of the township had passed away, and party branch structures had changed.

Today in Zambia the people we study demand—for example, in the voice of Commander Mpunga—a say in defining anthropology's research subjects. In my subsequent work, I have tried to reckon with the commander's plea to extend my gender focus across class to include persons of privilege as well as persons of lesser means. I find myself remembering his views on "the proper subject of study" whenever I learn of the frequent police clampdowns on women traders. The commander gave me the line of the past government and its single party: Zambia is an egalitarian society. It can point to a few women in prominent positions. Yet he was also painfully aware that things aren't always what they seem. Women who trade in public, such as those in the township I studied for many years, continue to be considered a nuisance. They are viewed ambiguously and blamed for the country's ills, ranging from scarcities and blackmarketing in the 1980s to, more recently, AIDS and cholera epidemics. "Development," the Commander said, "takes a lot of time."

Development does take a long time. I can think of few other persons who expressed more straightforwardly the challenge, and agony, of an anthropology of the present in postcolonial Africa. I shall never forget Commander Mpunga, who, in impeccable English and conversant with the language of social science research, made me account for myself and my purpose. Admonishing me as he did, he sought not only to shape my focus of study but also to reconfigure the role of the anthropologist. His apprehensions initially troubled me until I realized that he perceived me in terms of the material circumstances of a world into which only a few Zambians are fully integrated. Knowing something about that world from his stay in the United Kingdom, he demonstrated his anguished awareness of difference when comparing the position of women in Zambia and Britain.

Our mutual constructions, the commander's of me as yet another anthropologist from the West and mine of him as a high-level Zambian police officer, located us differently in the global setting that we were both part of. My participant observation in a low-income township did not break that perception. My research focus on poor women did not fit well into his construction of Zambia in national policy terms as a developing country in which things were bound to change for the better. Reminding me that there is a wealthier population segment, he insisted on a representation of society that did not look bleak. In the commander's double-edged reflections, Zambia slowly becomes more like the West at the same time as foreign anthropologists become sensitized to specific local needs, politics, gendered relationships, and much more. As a striking commentary on the gulf between formal political rhetoric and actual livelihoods, this interchange has helped to clarify my understanding of the uneasy relationship between the state and civil society in Zambia as well as of the ambiguous status Western anthropologists have in it. Perhaps we all need a Special Branch officer, or someone like him, to jolt our understanding of who we are and what we think we are doing.

Leaving My Father's House

AMITAVA KUMAR

Only one plane flew out from Patna during the afternoon. There were very few people around at the airport. Through the small window in the plane, I watched the rest of my family standing far back from the tarmac. They were all there to say good-bye to me, aunts and uncles; my mother in a new sari; my grand-mother, who had been brought from the village in which she lived; several cousins and their spouses; my brother-in-law; and a young nephew. I was a little nervous—getting the American visa hadn't been easy, and the fear remained that I would be turned back at any point—but I was also tremendously excited and happy.

It was a bright afternoon in August in 1986. I was leaving India for the United States to get a graduate degree. I couldn't stop reminding myself that it was the first time I had stepped on a plane.

Outside, it was hot. My grandmother and a few others from the family stood in the shadow of a small plane that was parked about fifty meters away. Although they were unable to see me, one or two of my relatives would raise their hand and wave. When the plane started moving, a cousin took off her long, scarf-like *dupatta* and held it with both hands so that an elegant span of bright orange unfurled in the strong breeze.

Then we were in the air. I removed from my hair the marigold leaves and grains of rice that my mother had sprinkled on me for good luck. Using the tip of her ring finger, my mother had put a spot of curd and red *sindoor* on the center of my forehead. I rubbed it off as I watched the attendant, young and smartly clad in a sari, slowly making her way down the aisle toward me.

It would be more than two years before I would be on a plane again. In December 1988, I was on my way back to India. I had received my master's degree; I was going on a two-week visit to my family. This time there was no one to see me off at this end in New York City. But, when I landed at the Indira Gandhi International Airport in Delhi, I found my father waiting for me. He had made the sixteen-hour journey from Patna by train to meet me when I was done with customs in the early hours of the morning.

We were to catch another train back to Patna very soon. We would also have to find time to visit my grandmother in the ancestral village. That first morning in Delhi, however, I needed to go to the Lufthansa office to confirm my flight back to the States. This didn't take long. We came out on the street, my father and I, and began to look for postcards. I had promised two friends that I'd drop them a line from India.

In the store, I found some cards I liked. I asked the middle-aged shopkeeper what I could pay him. He said the postcards cost three rupees. "That much?" I exclaimed in surprise. In 1986, when I had left, I was certain they were going for half that price. (Last year, I found out that prices have increased fivefold since then.) "This is quite expensive," I said to the shopkeeper.

"Not as expensive as where you are coming from," the man responded matter-of-factly. He didn't even bother to look at me.

I was suddenly angry. "And where am I coming from?" I asked him. But, the shopkeeper didn't think he needed to answer me. I looked at my father and he said, "Prices have gone up."

When we had paid and were out on the street again, I saw that my father was smiling. He said, "Woh jaanta tha tum baahar se aaye ho." (He knew you had come from outside.)

Had I changed? In only two years? Was this no longer my country, my home? It wasn't as if I hadn't contemplated questions of this nature before. Now, however, they seemed unexpectedly out of my control. Perhaps it had just struck me that even the answer to such questions lay not with me but with the shopkeeper, who hardly knew me but had the power to dispense judgment. This irked me more than the fact that he was right.

For his part, my father was interested in neither the questions nor their answers. They were not as important as the basic truth for him: his son had managed to go and live abroad—in the West—and was now recognized as such by the unknown shopkeeper.

And I?

I was entering the drama that was becoming the reality of thousands, no, more than a million, Indians. In a short story by Jhumpa Lahiri, this reality is summed up succinctly. In the story, we read the words of an Indian who had come to Boston as a young man on the day the Americans first landed on the moon: "While the astronauts, heroes forever, spent mere hours on the moon, I have remained in this new world for nearly thirty years. I know that my achievement is quite ordinary. I am not the only man to seek his fortune far from home, and certainly I am not the first. Still, there are times I am bewildered by each mile I have traveled, each meal I have eaten, each person I have known, each room in which I have slept. As ordinary as it all appears, there are times when it is beyond my imagination."

It is the children of the man in Lahiri's story who occupy the present. At the turn of the new millennium it is they who are our future.

In the new writing that is being done or the art that is being produced by Indians, we will need to recognize those who are being born in the diaspora—in the United States, England, and Canada or France, but also in Africa and the Caribbean—as the inheritors of our new modernity.

This reality hasn't made any conspicuous entry into the popular or dominant fiction that is given the name "Indian writing" in the United States and other places. The children of the Indian or Pakistani immigrants are only beginning to find their space in the work of writers like Hanif Kureishi and even Jhumpa Lahiri. There they emerge as the creative, volatile bearers of difference.

Their questions, even their confusions, fascinate me. One student in an undergraduate class at Yale, in the spring of 1999, wrote this on his first day: "I want to know how to read Rushdie, Naipaul, Roy, and others—are they really India? Are they Indian in the same way that I am? What is my relation to them? What is our relation to India?"

I await the answers that only they can give me.

* * *

On my first day in America, I ate beef and drank beer.

As I did that, and I'm not kidding, I remembered the story my mother had told me of Gandhi's struggle with meat in his youth. An older friend told Gandhi in high school that many of their teachers were secretly eating meat and drinking wine. In the state of Gujarat, because of the influence of Jainism in particular, there is an abhorrence for meat among Hindus. But Gandhi wanted to be strong and free of the fear of thieves and darkness.

He had been told that if he ate meat he would gain physical and psychological strength. In his autobiography, Gandhi tells us that there was even a doggerel by the Gujarati poet Narmad that was popular among boys: "Behold the mighty Englishman/ He rules the Indian small/Because being a meat-eater/He is five cubits tall."

A day was chosen by Gandhi and his friend. On a lonely spot by the river, Gandhi ate goat meat for the first time. He felt wretched and was unable to complete the meal. That night he was wracked by nightmares and remorse. Still, neither his friend nor Gandhi himself was willing to give up the experiment. Their surreptitious meals continued for over a year. Then, Gandhi decided he had no stomach for lying constantly to his mother about his meals. He gave up meat, saying to himself that he wouldn't eat it while his parents lived. He never ate meat again.

I had never eaten beef before in my life. Only once, on a visit to the southern Indian city of Hyderabad as a schoolboy, I had seen cow's meat being sold in the open. I was in a car with my parents and sisters. I turned to look at a large hunk of meat hanging in front of a butcher's kiosk. The driver, trying to perhaps make common cause—among Hindus—where none was needed, said, "This is a Muslim area. They wouldn't dare to sell beef anywhere else in the city."

I had turned my eyes away at the remark as if I needed to quickly erase the evidence my eyes had seen. I knew that religious riots between Hindus and Muslims often began with the killing of a cow or a pig and the carcass being thrown into a temple or a mosque to provoke a response. In my young mind, it was the possibility of religious violence that I was turning away from if I straightened my gaze and looked instead at the road ahead.

Now I was in America and it didn't matter. I remember thinking of my mother's story about Gandhi, but felt no overwhelming sense of guilt.

My companion was a friend who was also from my hometown, Patna. We had both gone to college in Delhi, and now he too had been admitted to the same university in Syracuse, New York. Two blocks from the apartment that we had found with the help of the International Students Office was a sandwich place that sold gyros and beef subs. I ordered beef because I wanted to know how it tasted. I had also decided I wasn't going to pretend I was still in India. I then asked for Heineken beer because I had seen it advertised in *Time* and other magazines sold in India. I had no dreams of bleating animals that Gandhi was plagued by.

If there was anything terrifying for me that first night in this country, it was the fear of failure, of never being able to become the scholar and writer that I wanted to be. I was quite convinced in my heart that although I had left home, even now the INS could send me home if I wrote terrible sentences.

Anyone could have told me that first night that I was indeed a failure. I was announcing to myself that I was free. But how? By drinking a bottle of Heineken!

If I wanted to console myself, I could have delusionally thought that I was failing like Gandhi—not because I didn't like the meat I was served, rather, I was finding out how I was defined by my past.

But I was only rehearsing earlier breaks and repeating other departures. I wanted desperately to believe that I belonged else-where. When I now think of that first day in this country, I am reminded of the time when I left Patna to go join secondary school in Delhi. I had recently won a scholarship. I took one of my mother's small steel trunks to the New Market in Patna and had it painted a shiny black. In bold letters in the right-hand corner, in white, I had the painter carefully write: A. KUMAR, NEW DELHI. To this day, some of my relatives call me by that whole "name."

I was sixteen then. The move had been made, I felt, from the provinces to the capital city. Suddenly, I wanted to be better at English and would write in a notebook all the unfamiliar words I encountered. The first entry in my notebook was the word "lambent." I had come across it, if memory serves me correctly, in Hardy's *Tess*.

Now, in America, I wanted to drink Heineken. That, too, was a debt to my past. The magazines in which I had seen the beer advertised were, as I have said before, used copies of *Time* and *Newsweek*. Those magazines were available for fifty paise in the chor bazaar, a flea market behind Delhi's Red Fort. I took the magazines home to my parents in Patna to show them that I was now a citizen of the world. Those magazines as well as the blue-gray school uniform in which I traveled back in the train to Patna were, for me, my own, distinctive signs of modernity.

Two more years passed in Delhi, and I cannot say exactly how, but those markers changed. I became interested in poetry, Marxism, and the Indian New Wave films. I was increasingly drawn by street plays and theater at the National School of Drama, the paintings of ordinary life that I saw coming out of Baroda, and the authors whose books I found in the Sahitya

Akademi Library, books that I would later recognize among the imports to the United States under the PL 480 program.

That was nearly twenty years ago. Most of those interests have stayed with me, and, as I think back, they give my life some continuity. One thing has changed, however. Now, when I walk on Delhi's streets, men walk up to me and ask me if I have any dollars to sell. I am recognized as an N.R.I., a non-resident Indian.

In Pankaj Mishra's *Butter Chicken in Ludhiana,* an account of his travels through small-town India, he describes meeting an Indian-American family "that had arrived some time back, filling the silent empty courtyard behind us with their twangy American accents and voluminous suitcases":

> Halfway through his spiel, Mr. Tomar was interrupted. It was the teenaged boy from the Indian-American family that had arrived some time ago.
>
> "Excuse me," he said, "may I have a boddle of Bissleri wadder?"
>
> A nonplussed Mr. Tomar looked at us first, and then, at him.
>
> "Sorry," he said, shaking his head in apology, "I didn't hear you."
>
> The boy repeated: "May I have a boddle of Bissleri wadder?"
>
> Mr. Tomar heard him attentively; then lunged at the only word he could guess at.
>
> "Oh, Bisleri!" he cried, "Yes, of course! How many bottles?"

And so it comes to me that I have become a part of a new stereotype, a stereotype of privilege. One that, when applied to Indians (especially writers) living abroad, proceeds, as Vikram Chandra recounts, in the following manner: "They are disconnected from Indian realities and are prey to nostalgia; and besides, the bastards are too comfortable over there and don't have to face Delhi traffic jams and power cuts and queues for phones and train tickets and buses, and so they don't suffer like us and they can't possibly be virtuous enough to be good artists."

* * *

Two years after coming to America, I moved to Minneapolis and enrolled in a Ph.D. program. I was living in a small, attic apartment—through the sloping roof close above my head, I heard the scurrying of animal feet as I slept—and would come down at rigidly prescribed hours to cook my meals. My landlady, who allowed me the use of her kitchen, was a recently divorced woman in her fifties. She lived alone, playing the piano and drinking martinis at night, and I was struck by the fact that she never ate the green olives she put in her drink. Before I moved to Minnesota, I had never seen an olive. Now, each morning, there were two or three plump olives lying discarded in the kitchen sink. On Saturdays, a Native American woman would come to clean the house. I cleaned my room myself, and I was permitted to do my laundry in the basement on weekdays.

One evening, I descended from the attic to cook supper after my landlady had eaten, as was my custom: rice and Progresso lentil soup, disguised with a few basic spices to taste a bit like dal. When I sat down at the kitchen table, I saw that the landlady—I had not thought of her until I started writing this, but I believe her name was Meg—had left the day's *New York Times* for me, with a blue arrow pointing to an article. The headline read: "Street Dramatist in India Slain Over Play." The story began: "A leftist who was one of India's most popular street theater directors was beaten to death by thugs last weekend after he refused a politician's demand to stop a drama in support of an opposing candidate, witnesses said."

The slain theater activist's name was Safdar Hashmi. I had watched his plays with great interest in India, before I came to this country; in the two years prior to his death, I had written poems with which I hoped to emulate the didacticism and the wit that were the hallmark of Hashmi's plays. I sat looking at the *Times* photograph of his corpse. Around him, illuminated by the light of the Delhi morning, stood many progressive intellectuals whose faces I recognized. I do not think I had ever felt as alone as I did that evening in my landlady's kitchen.

I will not claim that Safdar was a friend of mine, although I had exchanged greetings with him at the bus stop, or at his street performances at Delhi University. He had an easy charm and a handsome face, and his talent was legendary. He was only nine years older than me, and he had provided me a model for the writer I wanted to become in the future. Even in faraway Minneapolis, in the brief obituary, I caught a glimpse of what had made him so inspiring: "Mr. Hashmi was popular for brief, biting satires that made fun of corrupt politicians, policemen and businessmen, which drew laughter and cheers from large audiences of industrial workers. . . . His plays . . . moved from the propagandist dramas of the early 1970s to subtler themes." A month later that year, Khomeini was to place the *fatwa* on Rushdie's head, and I could only think of Safdar being bludgeoned to death on a road in Sahibabad outside Delhi. He was thirty-four years old—I remember noticing even in my shock that the *Times* reporter had got his age wrong—and now he was dead.

Safdar's killing unleashed a wave of grief and rage in India. The funeral procession was a nine-mile-long serpent of artists, workers, students—people from every fragment of a fragmented nation. The play that had been interrupted by his murder was performed on the first anniversary of his death in towns and cities throughout India. Safdar's widow, Moloyashree, acted in the play, when it was performed a few days after Safdar's death, at the very place where the actors had been attacked by thugs.

It was not until a few years later that I was made to think of all this again, in a new way. I had taken up my first job, teaching English in Florida, when, in 1997, Qamar Azad Hashmi published *The Fifth Flame,* an account of the life of her murdered son. The book's epigraph reads: "Four flames eternal burn at the shrine/I've come to set the fifth alight."

Reading the book from the distance of a migrant's self-inflicted isolation, I found that *The Fifth Flame* also made me nostalgic. This feeling was not the familiar yearning for the land of my birth or its people, but for a return to the social and political organizations that help literature transcend fantasy. As a writer, I began thinking of my differences from the one who was in some sense my hero.

Safdar Hashmi received his mail in the offices of the Communist Party of India (Marxist) in Delhi; most Indian writers who are discussed in the West have addresses only in the creative writing programs of American universities. Safdar thought of theater as that which "brings people closer to fighting organizations." Will the West's favorite Indian writers ever find institutions that can mobilize the South Asian community in the United States? Will the AFL-CIO come looking for the immigrant scribes to write about those who toil as cabdrivers, nannies, garment workers, and noncontract laborers? When will Safdar Hashmi come to America?

When I think back to the day when I first got on the plane, I know I only wanted to become a writer. Despite what I thought of as my political consciousness, this was still a private dream. Now, no longer. The ways in which I have tried to understand—perhaps even calculate—my loneliness have made me think long and hard about communities. There is an account of V. S. Naipaul talking to an editor about himself and his brother: "If we were addressing audiences of people like ourselves, we would have been different writers. I am always aware of writing in a vacuum, almost always for myself, and almost not having an audience. That wonderful relationship that I felt an American writer would always have with his American readers, or a French writer with his French readers—I was always writing for people who were indifferent to my material."

Ah, readers. . . . To think that a critical mass of the right kind of readers could have saved us from the truth of those words and, given the fact that Naipaul has often seemed to cultivate a Western audience, their lurking disingenuousness. That an audience of "ourselves" would have relieved us not only of the mannerisms, but also the desperate grasping for authenticity, in so much of what passes as Indian writing in the West. We would also have been rescued from undying nostalgia.

When writing of the West African *griot* songs, Manthia Diawara describes how they have trapped folks like himself "in a narrative of return": "We are kings in Mande, even if we wash dishes or clean toilets in other lands." The *griot*'s song offers a refuge to the exile, to "the new Mande heroes, who sweep the terrace of the Eiffel Tower and the streets of Paris, who drive cabs in Montreal or peddle African sculptures on 125th Street in Harlem." In other words, the *griot*'s song offers a life-long guarantee of a gesture, a pose of endless return. This is a fable of stable origin. Indian writers living in the diaspora partake of a little bit of that myth: like the African *griots,* even while we labor in the West, we re-create in one form or another the narrative of imagined return and imagined glory, blinding ourselves to the catastrophe all around us.

We need to face several sobering facts. A study at the beginning of the last decade had found that India had lost $13 billion to the developed countries by way of "brain drain" and the United States had gained $67 billion. Approximately 540,000 Indians had left India for the West by the end of the twentieth century. Rather than think of India as the Eden of my longing, I must think of it as a place I left; those whom I love and whom I have left behind, when they demand onions today, are given nuclear bombs instead. These are lessons in privilege. They introduce very quickly considerations of class, caste, gender, sexual choices, region, and religion. I think of the short poem "I'm Coming Home" by Bangladeshi writer Taslima Nasrin: "It was a pretty big deal, crowds of fascinated people applauded/in Paris, Strasbourg, Marseilles, Nantes." The poem, when read in its entirety, provides an inventory of the pleasures that await return, the porch of the house, the water-soaked rice, the fragrant *paan,* lemon groves, the newborn calf, the poet's mother's sweat, which recalls to her her childhood. The poem ends: "I've had lots of swims in the ocean, now I'll take two dips/at high noon in the village pond,/Nikhil-da." But this familiar landscape, eagerly anticipated and given graphic form in this poem, mocks the return of the poet in real life. Since her return to Bangladesh, Nasrin has been persecuted by ultranationalist, male Islamic fundamentalists and threatened with death. The imagined return remains just that—an imagined one.

* * *

Seven years after coming to the United States, armed with a worker's visa, I got a job at a university. Far away on the West coast, the state of California was engaged in debates over anti-immigration legislation. The annual Modern Language Association meeting was held in San Diego that year. I decided to go. During the week that I spent there, I took photographs at the border and talked to people, including officers for the Border Patrol. When the MLA conference was over, I got into my rented car and drove out of San Diego. Before night had fallen, I was in the desert. I was going to meet two friends who were spending their winter vacation in a cabin in the middle of the Mojave Desert. It was New Year's Eve.

There were Joshua trees all around us. My American friends had lit a bonfire on the open sands. The guests there, perhaps half a dozen or more, were asked to write down our wishes for the new year on slips of paper. We were then to throw the scraps on the fire. My hosts had fashioned for themselves elaborate scripts bound together with multicolored threads. A middle-aged man in a track suit flung on the flames what looked like a letter.

What was I going to do? From my car I took out my new Rand-McNally road map of the United States. I found the page that had the map of the state of Indiana and cut out only the part that said INDIA. Now that I had found work in this country and was getting ready to apply for a green card, I wanted to go back home to Patna. I wanted to write a book about the landless laborers from my ancestral village who migrated every summer to work in the rock quarries and wheat fields of Punjab. I had decided that they were the real migrants, not I. What did I know about the pains of leaving home to look for work? After all, I had a Rand-McNally road map with me. Also, unlike the workers who left the village in groups to catch a train that took them to the western plains in India over several days, I had a rented car. On its hood, right now, rested my gleaming glass of chianti. And besides, I was warm with the dream of being a writer.

Another guest, an older woman I had just met at the party, saw what I was doing to my road map. She laughed. "I so very much want to go to India," she said. "Our book club has been reading Vikram Seth's *A Suitable Boy.*"

It has become more and more common in the last few years for people to strike up a conversation with me about Indian writers in English. I am speaking, of course, of people in the West, mostly in the United States. We can be at a party, on a bus, or in an airport bookstore. The conversation so often begins or ends with my interlocutor asking me if I am Indian. Yes? Are you a doctor? Computer engineer? No, I teach English. Oh, I love Salman Rushdie! Or Vikram Seth, Arundhati Roy, Hanif Kureishi, Amitav Ghosh, Rohinton Mistry, Anita Desai. Once, I was asked if I was related to Hari Kumar in *The Jewel in the Crown* playing on PBS's *Masterpiece Theater.*

In my first few years in this country, I was incessantly quizzed about arranged marriages and bride burning. Suddenly it is more common now to be asked about novels. I guess one could regard that as a change for the better. In my own writing, especially the nonfiction that I write for the ethnic press in the United States, I try to present an inventory of our lived experiences. In fact, in an attempt to record what has been my own past, I feel I am practicing a self-ethnography that is not without interest to other immigrant writers. And, although I have learned a lot from them, I find evidence of our lives in more ordinary places than the writers I am incessantly quizzed about.

For example, while sitting in my doctor's clinic, I read in an old copy of the *New Yorker* that out of any five people who kill themselves, only one is likely to leave a note. The very next line in the report mentioned that immigrants to America are more likely to sign their names on their suicide notes than people who were born in this country.

That line set off a train of speculation in my mind.

The formality of the signed name at the end of a note—"Vimal Rao"—what would it explain about a man living with his wife and children in Connecticut for twelve years after emigrating from India?

Would the eldest daughter in the family coming upon a note written in her father's hand—the note beginning with the words "Dearest Shanti and my beloved children"—would the daughter need to make her way to the signed name at the end before realizing what had happened in the room whose door she had still not opened?

In another ten or fifteen minutes, a police car appears at their door. Perhaps the daughter thinks for a moment that if he were still here—her father, that is—he would have put on a shirt to answer the knock.

When in a hurry, he would often tuck the top button in the wrong hole. Actually, the daughter knows that when her parents fought, her father put on a shirt too. He did this because on such occasions he wanted to appear formal to her mother, as if to say the matter was now closed.

What that little detail—about immigrants signing their names on their suicide notes—what it had opened in me was an anxiety. I emigrated to this country thirteen years ago. Will I get to go home to die? Who will know me here?

Immigrants sign their names because they want to tell you who they are. This is who I was in this land, a stranger with a name.

There have been several reports in the papers recently about Indians living in the States. But, it is the reality of Indians also dying in this country that no one talks about.

Just a few months ago, the *New York Times* carried a report on middle-class *desi* immigrants flooding the American countryside. With a barely suppressed smirk, the reporter introduced the readers to one woman from India, a recent arrival who had been attending free English conversation classes and was able to tell him, "Bridgewater is very peaceful, very clean, very nice. We like it very much."

But, where are the stories about the problems of dying in this country? What happened to the poor bastard from Surat who got caught in the cross fire in Queens? "Forget the strangers," I want to say to my fellow *desis*. "Let's talk about yourselves. . . . Where are the stories about you when you heard of the death of your loved ones in India while you were here in the US?"

I am not asking such questions from an excess of sentimentality. These are undeniably also practical questions.

When a close friend's father died in Calcutta recently, I waited for my friend's return from India to ask him how he had managed to get an air ticket so quickly. It turned out that Air India, for example, claimed that all of its flights were full; my friend was able to find a place after much uncertainty because his own brother is a travel agent. What will happen to me in the same situation?

A couple of years ago, I was reading my poetry on a panel with several other South Asian authors. One of my fellow panelists read a short story in which a Hindu man who has died in this country is being given a farewell at a ceremony organized in a church.

Suddenly, I was reminded of a boyhood memory from Patna. My history teacher had died of cirrhosis of the liver when I was in the sixth grade. Just before he died, my teacher wrote a letter to the eldest Jesuit at the school, asking him to ensure that he was cremated rather than get a burial, as was his due as a Christian. It turned out that the teacher had been a Hindu earlier; he had converted, perhaps, to fit in better in his place of work, and now wanted to go home to the religion of his birth.

It is possible that I had given a communal color to the story as I heard it in my boyhood, and that is the reason why I have narrated it as I have above. As you can see, it had become in my young mind a story about a man returning to the fold. It is possible that is how the story was repeated to me by the senior students or our parents.

In any case, as I think back to the short-story writer reading her tale in New York and to the story from my boyhood, I ask myself whether I shouldn't temper my anxiety. If I were to die here today, then indeed, just as I live here, I should also be prepared that my friends and colleagues will take care of my remains here. As immigrants, our lives convey an inescapable mixing: I once attended an Indian wedding in a small-town mall in Florida. My ancestors, I can be sure, never stepped inside a church. But, I should be happy to get a dignified and decent farewell in my neighborhood church, which, I have to admit, appears to have a fine-trimmed garden and would look pleasant on a winter afternoon, even to a dead man.

Miguel Alemán and His Dam

BEN FEINBERG

My wife told me about this wedding in Santa Rosa. At first, I did not want to go. I thought about the screaming babies and everybody standing around. I thought about my wife making me dance Flor de Naranjo against my will for hours. I thought of the long ride. But only for a minute.

"What the hell, let's go," I said. I was looking forward to it. I had never been to Santa Rosa, and I had a godson there named Victor. This kid had come to live with us for a year when he was just a little thing. I guess I shouldn't call him a kid; he must be almost thirty now. It would be nice to get out into the country, to see the Sierra as it should be seen and pass the time with some good friends. And besides, my wife's mother wasn't going. So nobody was going to be ordering me around, ordering everyone around, making me wait.

We found out that some businessman was driving out in that direction, all the way to Rio Seco, and arranged to ride in his truck. My wife rode in the cab with the baby and Luisa, our youngest daughter. I rode in the back with my son Manuel, my mother, and my mother's *comadre* Maria, an ancient old grandmother—we called her grandmother because she was so old—

with a creaky laugh and one scraggly tooth on the upper gum that hung down over the teeth on the lower gum. Manuel kept hanging his feet over the side. "Get your feet in here," I said, over and over again. "You're going to fall out of the truck." I don't have much faith in Manuel. He's a nice enough kid, and plenty smart, but he doesn't like to work. That would be fine, I suppose, if he studied, but he doesn't do that either. He just spends all his time out in the street playing with his friends, like he's going to be fifteen years old forever. And he's disobedient. You could say that I've already given up on Mani. Maybe the other kids will make something of themselves. Little Marcos likes to work all right—he already makes some money every morning washing the buses—and there's always the baby. Maybe the girls will marry well. I was glad the other kids weren't coming on this trip.

Maria named all the places we passed on the two-hour ride to Santa Rosa, every creek and mountain ridge and cluster of houses. That's the cliff of frogs, she said at one point, waving off to the right. There are many caves there, many caves. The people went to live in the caves at the time of the Revolution to hide from the soldiers. It was a time of great fear for the people, great fear.

I tried to imagine living in a cave. It sounded cramped and moist. I guessed that it would depend on how big the cave was, especially with a large family. Since we were going to a wedding, and since I felt like saying something, I asked Maria how she met her husband. She laughed, that funny croaking noise. Eh heh heh. I met him when we were married. I was from a little rancho, but I married in Huautla. Before the people never met their husband or wife until the wedding. It was all arranged. The parents of the groom would come to the house of the bride to ask permission from the parents of the bride. They would bring beans and corn and cane liquor. Everyone asked for permission then. Not like now. It's different now.

I knew that, of course, but still I had asked the question. I probably asked it just to keep her from naming places, to get her to talk about something else. But still, the idea of committing oneself to live until death with a stranger seemed frightening, a nightmare. Weren't there a lot of problems? I asked. Since they didn't know each other. What if they didn't get along? Of course, I thought about my own wife in the cab, who wouldn't give me anything since the operation after the baby, since God only wants it for procreation or some priest shit line like that, and how she was always bitching. And I *chose* her. I was no one to talk. We had our good years though, back when we lived at the ranch, before the second or third kid.

Maria creaked again. "Oh no," she said. The marriages went well, usually. I asked how her marriage went. She said that it went fine and they had three children. Except that her husband drank too much and died young, at twenty-two or twenty-three. But I was like the women now, she said. I only had three children. Before we used to have ten or twelve. Everybody.

"Like dogs," said my mother, who had ten. "Like animals," said Maria. Like burros. The two old women giggled like schoolgirls. "Get your feet inside the truck," I told Manuel.

I thought about what it would be like to be as old and creaky as Maria, and to ride in the back of a truck. It was not an unpleasant thought, and I knew that some day that would be me, my life, and it would be just fine, better than now. And the truck bounced high on another rock or pothole on this rutted roadway recently gouged from this particularly stony section of mountain and lifted me up off my seat as if to place me, now, half a lifetime ahead of schedule, in the place of María where I could look back and serenely mock the life courses of myself and others, and I was ready, God knows, I was ready to be a *viejito*. I will have no more children, and no more good will come from my land. But I landed hard back on my narrow metal seat in the endless middle years of life, while Maria and my mother seemed to hover in the air an additional moment before smoothly floating down into the same rough conditions that had treated my backside with considerably less dignity. "You're going to fall, idiot," I told my disobedient foolish son. He was smiling.

The sun was shining in Santa Rosa when we got there around noon, and we could see all the way up to Pico de Orizaba, the snow-covered, tallest volcano in Mexico, in one direction, and all the way down to the Miguel Alemán lake in the other, full of islands, the sun dancing on the water's surface. A nearby hill blocked our view of most of the lake, but it still looked beautiful, and I said so. "It would look better from that mountain," said Manuel, pointing at the hill. "I'm going to go up there." "Shut up," I told him. "You're not going anywhere. Let's go see your *compadres*."

My wife was bitching about something, about how the kid wouldn't sleep and kept crying. "He's sick," she said. "I'll have to go find a doctor." "Leave it alone," I said. "He'll be all right." We went down to the house of the bride. The businessman decided to stay for the party and came with us, leaving the truck parked along the road. The father of the bride was already very drunk, as was his youngest brother, my godson Victor. "How good that you have come," said the father, and they offered me and the businessman beers and brought a soda for Manuel. The women disappeared into the kitchen. We talked, and I had a shot of mescal and a beer, and smoked two cigarettes. It was good to talk to my godson after all these years. He was working in Mexico City now, as an assistant to a taco vendor in a metro station. Everyone in Santa Rosa, it seemed, lived in Mexico City, and everyone at the party would be in town for only a few days. Even the groom planned to delve into that mysterious but fruitful metropolis with his new bride, two days after the wedding.

But mostly we stood there waiting for something to happen, just a bunch of men in a room with a dirt floor and one long table covered by a plastic pink and white tablecloth. It was only morning, and all of the men of the bride's family were far into the celebration, like I said. "It's great to see you Bernardo, nardo," said the bride's father. "You know what? I'm a *cabrón*." I didn't disagree with his self-assessment or challenge his mistake about my name, but smiled and accepted a cup of *aguardiente* and congratulated him on his daughter's marriage. "God damn," he said. "I respect you, you know that. I goddamn respect you, *cabrón*. Because you're a *cabrón*." We sat at the table and some women came and served us bowls of delicious goat soup, a piece of meat or an organ floating in spicy brown broth. Mani told me he wasn't hungry, and he didn't like goat meat anyway. The boy's a Huauteco, a Maza-teco for God's sake, and says he doesn't like goat meat. I had had just about enough. "Sit down," I said. But Manuel was out the door. During the meal nobody said anything. We just sat there and ate the soup with tortillas, lifting the bowls to drink the broth. It was delicious, but I didn't say so. I just said "Provecho" when I was done and stood up, and the other men grumbled back at me.

The procession was about to start now, from the house of the bride to the church, and my wife was not about, but this didn't cause me any alarm. Let her go where she wants, it's no concern of mine. Better that she stays out of my way.

But then, as the line of men (in back) and women sand-wiched the musicians snaking their way up the hill toward the church, she came hobbling up, clutching the allegedly sick baby, my last gasping attempt at immortality. She eyed me, but spoke to my mother. I could hear the words, though.

"It is his stomach," she said. She said that his stomach ached him because his father—she looked my way, and continued to look my way—because his father gave him a glass of soda pop first thing in the morning, before he had eaten anything else. She said that this was what the doctor had told her, that she walked all the way up the road in the sun, carrying the creature. She said the doctor had given her two pills. She said that it tired her greatly to see to all the baby's needs, and that she could not trust him to his father because he doesn't think.

My mother smiled like an old burro and shook her head.

"Look dear," I said. "The procession is reaching the church. Let's go."

Inside the church, about half of us sat at the pews and listened to the priest talk and sing, accompanied by a teenage guitarist. Outside, the rest of us stood around with the young couple lis-tening to the *mariachis* play their grungy, drunken, traditional songs—which drowned out the priest's blather, even inside the building, annoying the old fellow immensely, or so I gathered from his occasional scowl in our (I belonged to the outside half of us) direction. I spotted Mani climbing on the side of the church. "Get down," I said. I don't know where he went, but it was quite some time before I saw him again, after the mass, sucking on a Peñafiel. Between those two episodes, I successfully managed to avoid thinking about my son the failure.

It was time to get going. The bride's father let us all know. "Vamonos cabrones," he shouted, and a fat young lady and a sweating young man stepped into the crumbling house of God and began a new life together. The little fat girl is pretty, I said to the man at my left. She will make a good wife.

The priest droned on and on. I didn't recognize him—he wasn't one of the priests from Huautla. I was glad that it wasn't Father José María. He's a good priest in many ways. He's always good to talk to and he does a good job with the mass, but he is always injecting politics into the service, talking about the *zapatistas* and the bad government and this or that. That's all fine, I guess, but when I go to church for Sunday mass, I don't want to hear about politics, which is all a bunch of lies to divide and deceive the people. And some, the ignorant, are fooled. The Father is *cabrón,* they say. How *chingón* Father is. I feel like telling them, Oh sure, he has pretty words. But go follow him. Go off and start some revolution and see what happens. You will be the first to die, shot down by soldiers who don't play around, and he'll slide on through to keep on talking, everybody's favorite, probably coming out on the other side much richer. Just keep on talking. How *chingón.* Just wait and see. But this priest wasn't José María.

My daughter squirmed in the seat next to me, and off and on I paid attention to what this unknown priest said, now that I was sitting inside and the young lovers stood at the front of the aisle, patiently listening to every word, maybe. He was explaining the differences between marriage in the holy Catholic Church and marriage by the lesser authority of the civil law. First, he said, the

Catholic Church will only marry women who are sixteen years or older and men who have accumulated eighteen years, while the law will prostitute its blessing to any girlchild of fourteen and boy of sixteen. The church refuses to do this because it believes that one must achieve a certain degree of maturity before committing oneself to a lifelong partner, a maturity that is only manifested at sixteen, for women, and eighteen for men.

I noticed that a dog had curled up under my seat and that another, a black male with white spots, trotted about sniffing, presumably searching for its hidden playmate, whose position was known only to me. I restrained myself and did nothing, while the priest, apparently in no hurry, slowly explained the second difference between church and civil regulations.

The law, said the priest, allows divorce, while the church does not. Once one is married before God, in the house of God, one is married forever and ever and the Lord does not accept any severance of this sacred bond. Where once there were two, there becomes one. The husband and wife cannot keep any secrets from each other, nor can they keep separate financial identities or any individual possessions. That is not marriage. That is not allowed. These representatives of separate families that undertake this alliance become one family, indissoluble, for as long as they both shall live. That is the teaching of the church.

I kicked the dog, which had probably brushed against me, and it yelped and ambled into the aisle. The other dog came chasing after it, tail wagging. My mind wandered away from the dronings of the priest, although I paid enough attention to kneel when it was time to pray and rise and hum along when it was time to sing. At some point rings and vows were exchanged, and we all staggered out into the sun to join the second round of festivities, as if this interlude, which was, after all, the whole point of the celebration, the most important event that would ever happen in the lives of two of us, had never occurred.

Tradition says that the big party after the church ceremony takes place at the house of the groom, and that is where my wife was heading. I didn't want to go up there, though. I knew that some people would still be at the house of the bride, including my *compadres,* and felt no desire to sweat and dance with *huipil*-clad old ladies in an overcrowded hut full of strangers. My wife told me to come. "No," I said, "it's no good up there, it's ugly. It's better at the house of the bride. Let's go there." "You go there," she said. "I'm going to the party, and you will come up later to watch the baby, because I can't take care of him all afternoon." "Very well," I said, and went back down the hill to the house of the bride, with Pico de Orizaba still gleaming behind me and the lake still awaiting far away in the distance ahead, calling me like a whistle, or so it seemed.

About twelve men, including most of the bride's family, shared my sentiments about the house of the groom and returned to the lower party. I wager that some of them had never left. I wandered over toward a heavyset young man wearing thick-rimmed glasses, the only fellow among this motley collection to possess these contraptions, a man who seemed a little less intoxicated than everyone else. I introduced myself, and before he could respond I recognized him as a son of Felipe Carrera, the last of the infamous Carrera bandits, who had gone out with such a splash at a wedding just six years ago in Santa Catarina.

I was there, since the bride was from Huautla, the niece of a *compadre,* and I saw the whole thing. Felipe had terrorized Santa Catarina and San Miguel, worse even than his uncle or his monstrous grandfather, who would throw the bodies of the travelers he robbed and killed into the bottomless caverns and sinkholes of that part of the Sierra. Nobody knows how many men and women Don Felipe killed, but he always went about armed, and whenever he approached town he found all the houses closed and dark and all the people hidden inside. Felipe controlled the *aguardiente* factory of Santa Catarina at that time, as he controlled just about everything else, and his thirst for strong cane liquor was as legendary as his cruelty and his unpredictable rages.

It so happened that Felipe and a number of other men had been drinking at the wedding six years ago and became unusually excited by the energetic playing of the *mariachis* who had been hired by the groom's father. No one remembers who started it, but soon three or four men, including Felipe, were firing their pistols in the air and whooping. I scurried away from these men and stationed myself behind a tree, for I had a feeling that something was about to happen. A man from Huautla named Don Fausto walked over to a truck and then returned. He spoke to Felipe. "I have a gun too," he said. "I have a gun too, you son of a bitch." And he shot Felipe in the chest, wounding him fatally. But the Carreras do not die quickly, like other mortal men, since they possess, or possessed, in those days, an extra soul borrowed from one of the Devils they serve. Felipe opened the leather coat he was fond of wearing, revealing not only the gaping wound but also four additional holsters and four guns. He fired into the crowd of men, killing Fausto and three others, including the father of the bride, before he died. Not even his mother grieved at his death. "He never knew," she said. "He never understood."

His son introduced himself. I asked what he was doing these days, and he said that he was working as an accountant for a coffee company, that he had finished school in Oaxaca. He said that he liked the city because of the concerts and the movies, but it was always nice to visit the mountains where he grew up. He said that he was only going to stay in this office a year or two and then he was going to go back to school so he could get a better job. He asked about me and I said, well, you know, I'm a campesino, the same as always. You know how that is.

I felt like going outside for a second. I felt like I should make sure that my son wasn't getting in any trouble. On my way out, I stepped over a man who had passed out in the doorway. White foam bubbled from his mouth and slowly migrated across his cheek. I noticed that the man was Alfonso Reyes, the oldest son of the late Don Fausto. I did not worry, since I was sure that he would not recognize the son of his rival.

Mani was sitting on the bench outside, drawing formless pictures in the dirt with a stick.

"Let's go," I said to Manuel. "Let's go up to that mountain there and look at the lake. I'll bet it looks more beautiful from there."

"Mom will be looking for us," he said. "Are we going?"

"Yes," I said.

Victor wobbled out of the house. "Godfather Ricardo," he said. He reached out with his arm. He stared into the sun and then at me. He pulled me back into the house. "Godfather Ricardo," he said. "How good that you came here to be with us. Come drink a little beer with me." Someone else pulled a Corona out of the case and opened it. They passed the beer to me. "Salud," said Victor. "Salud," I mumbled. I pressed the beer to my lips and looked toward the door. Manuel stood there. He lowered his head and walked away. Vic said something that I didn't understand. "That's OK," I said. "How good that I can share this beer with my godson and my *compadres* on this day of happiness." Eduardo, the father of the bride, was sitting on the bench, spitting onto his pant's leg. "Compadre Ricardo," he said. "Come here and talk a moment with me." Cabrones. Everywhere in the room there were men, and they were reaching out toward me and saliva was dribbling from their lips. There weren't any women at this party, except for the ones in the kitchen. There was no dancing and no musicians, just music from a tape player. "I have to leave a signature," I said. And then I almost screamed, "I have to piss."

I went outside and saw Manuel sitting on a bench. He was digging in the ground with his fingers. My lazy son who will never amount to anything, who doesn't like to study and doesn't like to work. Who thinks that all of life is a game.

"Let's go," I said. "This way so nobody sees us."

In a moment we were back on the road. We walked rapidly through the town until we came to a path that led down to the left, toward our goal. We headed off on the path, past many houses, until there weren't very many houses at all. Occasionally little narrow trails veered off of our path. I knew that these led to other, isolated houses full of people. We kept going.

"How will we know when we get there?" asked Manuel. "We'll know," I said. We were walking along the mountain's side, with the ridge to our right. "Stop," I said. "Look back." Behind us we could see Santa Rosa. The blue paint on the larger houses gleamed in the sun. I hadn't noticed before that almost every building in town was painted blue. There wasn't a cloud in the sky. Above the town we could see the white summit of Pico de Orizaba far, far away. "There's the church," I said, "where the wedding was. And there's the party at the bride's house. And up there, where the smoke is, that is the house of the groom. Santa Rosa looks good from here, eh?"

My son said, "Yes, it looks *padre* from here." He asked where the truck was. I couldn't see it. "Behind those trees," I said. "Just above the house of the bride."

We continued and turned off onto a trail leading up the side of the mountain. My son followed me. We came to an intersection. Straight ahead I saw that the trail led to a house, and children were playing and screaming outside. We went to the right, up the mountain. I could feel all the cigarettes that I had smoked at the party. I could feel that I wasn't a young man anymore. We kept climbing up the mountain, the two of us.

The trail ran into a little house and ended. The door to the house stood open and two dogs were sniffing each other in front, the lackluster and mechanical sniffing of dogs that must already know each other intimately, dogs that have nothing better to do. I saw where we could reach the top of the ridge, but to get there we would have to cross the cleared area in front of the house, the flat place where soon, God willing, the residents will dry their coffee beans. We crossed, and a dog ran toward us, barking.

"Hello," I called into the house. There was a response, a female voice. "We are crossing here to go up the mountain," I said. "Go ahead," a woman responded. I was looking directly into the house, but I didn't see any adult women. Just children, three of them. Manuel threw a rock at the dog and it ran back, still barking, its tail between its legs.

Now we were walking where there was no trail, but the way was clear, up over the rocks, and soon we stood on a flat out-cropping where we could see all the way down to the lake. It looked like it was a thousand kilometers away, but at the same time as clear as if it were just over the next ridge. The lake was full of islands, hundreds of them. "Look, there's a bridge," said Manuel. "No," I said, "that's not a bridge. It's the difference in temperature in the water. The darker parts are colder, or maybe warmer, or deeper. But it's not a bridge."

We stood there admiring the view, leaning against a young palm tree—a palm tree in the Sierra! How did it get there? We stood there for a while. I knew that my wife was probably search-ing all over Santa Rosa for me, from one party to another, up and down, for no reason other than to scold me for being out of sight. I didn't care. I told my son about the lake.

"Once there were many people down there," I said. "Many cattle. It was a ranching zone. There people lived and raised cat-tle and goats and sheep. There were towns there. Then, in the time when Miguel Alemán was President of the Republic, they built a dam and filled it up with water. The poor people had to leave. Some didn't leave, and drowned. Your grandfather was born there. He was a young man, just barely older than you when they filled it with water, and so he came to Huautla to live. It was hard for him, and he had to fight to survive. But that, over there, is where our race comes from. Our ancestors lived and died there for hundreds of years—who knows how long? They are buried beneath the water in a cemetery no one will ever visit."

We stood there admiring the view for a while, looking at the islands and the different colors in the water and the yellow line on the far shore and the brightness of the reflected sunlight. We didn't see any people at all; no towns or fishing boats, just peace and tranquillity and beauty.[1] They told me later that the bride, who was fifteen, didn't know the man she was marrying, that it was an arranged marriage. That at the party she sat at the other end of the room and would not look at him or talk to him. God, it's horrible.

NOTE

1. Alternative happy ending: On the way back I encountered an older man
   dressed in white *calzones*. I pointed toward the lake and asked him the name
   of a village we saw in the distance. Was it San Pedro, or Nguixui, as we call it?
   No, he said, Nguixui is behind that hill, which is called Taukaa. That village
   is Ndaxali. And I asked what lay behind another hill, to the right of Ndaxali,
   and he thought a moment, and told me. And we stood there, looking off
   toward the lake, pointing at various places—houses, creeks, hills, and
   valleys—and calling them by their names.

The Battered Wife's Tale

LAUREL KENDALL

Sometimes a story squeezes through the narrow apertures of an interviewer's agenda and presents itself, unexpected, fully formed, and unforgettable, the urgent presence of something that must be told, shared, acknowledged. I have written of how the shaman, Yongsu's mother, utterly subverted my attempts to conduct a simple household survey: "When we asked about marriage, the dam burst and the words poured out, rising and falling until the tale was told" (Kendall 1988, 19). The force of that flood swept me into writing *The Life and Hard Times of a Korean Shaman*. Yongsu's mother was a dominant presence in my life. Her stories punctuated nearly two years of fieldwork, and her voice was loud in my head during the years that I wrestled with the book she had all but willed me to write. The story I am about to retell does not have this history. I heard it in a single morning during an interview with a woman I never saw again. This interview haunted me for many years, but far from feeling empowered to write about it, I have wondered whether I ought to write it at all.

In the autumn of 1987, I was in Seoul interviewing matchmakers for a book on late twentieth century Korean matrimony.

My small team of researchers was charged with the responsibility of finding matchmakers among their mothers, mother's friends, and relations and arranging for them to talk with me about their experiences. Misuk was one of my assistants, a recent graduate of a not-so-prestigious university. She would telephone and tell me to meet her at one or another unfamiliar outlying subway station and then lead me to a modest apartment or threadbare tearoom where I would conduct one more interviews with an amateur matchmaker.

On this misty September morning, we meet at Tongjak Station, south of the Han River. Misuk arrives, slightly out of breath, and without pausing to elaborate on where we are going, sets a brisk pace across an empty, park-like space and through residential streets. We walk a great distance, Misuk with only plastic shower clogs on her feet. From the clogs, and the fact that she is not carrying her usual handbag and notebook, I realize that we are going to her own home.

Although real estate developers have turned Seoul south of the river into a forest of high-rise buildings, Misuk's neighborhood, up a steep hillside, is of another time, a cluster of small Korean-style houses, vegetable patches, and even a few trees shading narrow walled courtyards. Misuk's mother is a pleasant, middle-aged woman whose face crinkles into a smile when we arrive. She is sitting in her glassed-in veranda with a young neighbor, a thin, delicate woman with unruly hair, dressed for housework in a shapeless skirt and bulky sweater. The young woman has a fidgeting baby in her arms.

What is Misuk's plan? Is her mother going to tell me about her own matchmaking experiences? Am I supposed to interview the young mother? Matchmaking is a preoccupation of the middle aged, but the young woman could be an amateur matchmaker. Misuk has already introduced me to a former classmate who arranged a successful match. Or has this young woman simply stopped by to gossip with a neighbor?

We exchange pleasantries. Misuk serves the juice and cookies that I have brought. The pendulum clock on the veranda bongs the hour. The young woman turns her pale face to me and says, "Ask your questions." Questions—I have a battery of questions. So she is my matchmaker. I clear my throat. "You've done matchmaking?"

I come from Pusan. A granny arranged my marriage. My husband was so disreputable that no one would marry him. I lived in the countryside before I got married, and he lived in the city.

I shift gears, begin a different batch of questions, the ones I ask when my subjects are recently married women. "Who was the matchmaker? What was her relationship to you?"

The granny was my mother's elder sister, and when she told the groom's family that she knew of a good young woman, they asked her to matchmaker for them. She was sympathetic to my mother-in-law's request. The son was in such bad shape that it would have been difficult to marry him off in Seoul.

"She was deceived," Misuk's mother states, quietly but firmly. Now I understand. Because I am "interested in matchmaking," Misuk and her mother have decided that I should hear this story of matchmaking gone horribly wrong.

My mother-in-law was anxious to marry him off. She thought that if he were married he might get a grip on his violent outbursts and wild demands for cash.[1] She thought that a Seoul woman would flee from that kind of man, but that a countrywoman would endure it. Besides, she thought that a countrywoman would be hard working and have a simple and honest disposition. . . .

I ask if I can turn on my small and unreliable tape recorder. "Is this for some broadcast network?" she asks.

Once again, an anthropologist is mistaken for a journalist. I am used to this. "No, no, this is for my research, so I can listen again later. Korean is difficult for me to understand. If I write about you someday, it will be in English and I will hide your identity."

She continues to speculate about a broadcast. "If my children's daddy heard it, he would be furious. I would really be in for it. Of course it won't matter if I decide to get divorced. You could broadcast it then. . . ."

Again, I insist that I am not a journalist, that I want to hear about her experiences so that I can broaden my understanding of matchmaking in Korea. I am curious now, anxious to hear her story. I ask another standard interview question: "Did you have other arranged meetings before you met your husband?"

I went to many arranged meetings. . . . My mother would only reach a decision after she had gone to a diviner. I had no recourse but to keep on seeing a certain man [from an arranged meeting] *until she got the* [unfavorable] *results. . . . My father said that since the courtship had gone so far, we had to go through with it. He insisted on it. All this dithering would only give rise to rumors and nothing good would come of it.*

She is already into her story, and she will tell it to the end, even as she pats and comforts her squirming baby, gives the child her breast, and, at one point, removes diapers, opens the sliding door, and positions the child to relieve itself over the courtyard.

I was about to be married. Just on the day before we were to receive the formal request of marriage (from his family), my maternal aunt showed up out of the blue. My mother let my aunt know that even though things had gone so far, she wasn't comfortable with the arrangement, her heart wasn't in it. Immediately, my aunt said that there was a fine bachelor in Seoul and that she had been asked to arrange a marriage for him with a suitable young woman. My mother told her to go right back up to Seoul and arrange a meeting with that man. Without pausing for so much as an hour to rest, my aunt dashed back up to Seoul.

They agreed to it in Seoul. As for us, it sounded too good to be true. Of course we trusted my aunt. She wasn't just anyone. She was my mother's sister. One would expect her to take great pains over her niece's wedding. Besides, my aunt was not one to take marriage lightly. There was no reason for us to be suspicious.

While all this was going on, I was out working in the peach orchard. I hadn't any idea that Mother had sent my aunt back to Seoul. When my mother said that she had gone so far as to send them my picture [to initiate matchmaking], *I didn't feel right about it. Since this was what my parents had done, I had faith in them and*

*followed their wishes. For my part, I wasn't particularly happy
about the man with whom I was going to finalize my engagement,
but other people had made the arrangement. I'd met with him, and
over time, I'd discovered his good qualities and thought that I might
have a good life if I married him. It wasn't that my mother didn't
like him so much as that she thought he wasn't good enough for us*
[probably because he was a farmer, by then a highly undesirable
groom]. *That was why, on the very day before we would finalize it,
she sent her sister up to Seoul with my picture.*

*That evening, we called my suitor's family and asked them not
to deliver the formal request of marriage because something had
happened in the family. . . . You can't just bluntly rebuff an offer of
marriage. . . . If you say words like, "Something has happened so let's
postpone it," they'll take your meaning as, "Oh, they don't want it."*

[Her aunt returned from Seoul the following afternoon with
the bachelor and his mother.] *In Korea, the greatest distance is
from Seoul to Pusan. I was startled that they had come all that way
on my account, to see me on the strength of just having seen my photograph. Isn't it natural that I should have felt grateful toward them
because they had done this on my account? I was overwhelmed. And
when there's a marriage prospect, the woman's side wants to make a
good impression. We didn't dare ask them about this and that after
they had come all this way to see me. All I could do was blush. It's
human nature. I wanted to believe everything, I didn't want to
doubt them.*

*In my aunt's telling, all of the conditions were favorable. I'm only
a high school graduate. In the countryside, that's not so bad, but the
groom was a college graduate, living well, and had an amicable per-
sonality. . . . My (future) father-in-law was a retired lieutenant
colonel. Everything seemed fine. My mother-in-law appeared to be
warm hearted and understanding and made a good appearance. My
future husband also gave the impression of being normal and healthy.
At that moment, I was so glad that they had come.*

*They ate supper at our home. They say that when the groom's side
looks the bride's side over, and if all of the conditions are favorable,
then when the groom is served dinner, if he likes us and is of a mind*

to get married, he should eat every last grain of rice. But if he is the least bit uncomfortable with the idea or has no intention of getting married, then he should leave it in his bowl. That's what they say, and he ate it all up, even drank every last drop of water. Since they had come from Seoul to look me over, the neighborhood grannies had all come over to our house to see what was going on. They laughed and said that he'd really polished the meal off in a hurry. The bachelor laughed and my (future) mother-in-law laughed with them. [The memory still produces a smile.] . . . *As she was leaving to catch the night train, my mother-in-law invited us up to see their home and set the date with my father for the next Sunday.*

I write in my fieldnotes that she is changing her child's sodden diapers when she tells me this, but that she does not interrupt the flow of her story. After this auspicious beginning, she went up to Seoul with her father to receive her first intimation that something is amiss.

When you tell someone to visit you, you ought to be at home. We arrived at Seoul Station with just their address—I'd asked the groom to write it down for me. We called, but no one was at home. That was strange. We doggedly took a taxi to their neighborhood and . . . searched high and low for their house.[2] We searched and searched. Worn out, I began to get angry. It hurt my pride. If something had come up, they should at least have left someone at home to answer the telephone since, after all, they had invited us. My anger rose as I searched. . . . I asked at this house and at that house and then leaned against someone's wall while my father continued to look for their house. Then, fortunately, the proprietress of a little hole-in-the-wall store told us that it was the house right in front of us and pointed to their front gate.

We knocked on the gate and a man came out and asked who we were. "We're from Pusan." He told us to wait and went inside. Maybe he tidied up. He seemed not to know where to put us. He said, "This is (the bachelor's) room," and the three of us sat down. He said that they had completely forgotten about our appointment. My future mother-in-law had gone off somewhere, the bachelor was somewhere else, no one was at home, my future father-in-law had himself just come back from an appointment. What if he hadn't come back early?

[Wanting to leave the two men alone to talk, and feeling exhausted from the search, she takes a nap in her future sister-in-law's room.] *I opened my eyes with a start when someone awakened me. It was my mother-in-law, who had come back home before the others. It was seven-thirty, almost supper time, so she fixed and served the meal. When I asked where she had gone, she said that she'd gone off in a hurry to deal with a sudden infestation of bugs in her grapevines. I told her how we had wandered around for such a long time looking for them. . . .*

We ate supper and talked past ten o'clock, but even then that bachelor hadn't returned. He seemed to be very busy. Since the last train was at ten-thirty, we left and came back home on train tickets my father-in-law had purchased for us. My father had taken to my future father-in-law right away and was pleased with the way they were living. I just followed suit, thinking that once I was married, then everything would be fine.

One week later, their side took all the initiative, even to setting the wedding day and bringing the betrothal gifts. When they brought me a diamond ring, a gold ring, a diamond necklace, a bracelet, and a Korean dress [as betrothal gifts], *I received these things with a feeling of deep gratitude. . . . The bachelor spent three or four days at our house and told me to come up to Seoul and see them. When he left, I promised that I would be up in a week.*

A week later, I went to Seoul by myself, spent a day, and came back home. But when I was at my [future] *husband's house, he didn't act the least bit like a man who had asked a woman for a date. It was strange. He barely said anything. Since I'm very bashful myself, I thought that he was just being shy. I wasn't at all suspicious.*

Only a short time after that, we were married. The wedding was in Seoul. Pusan was too far away for them. We sent 3,500,000 wôn up to Seoul for dowry goods. They had suggested that it would be easier if they just bought everything in Seoul. Since we were busy with transplanting rice, we sent the money up to the groom's family. Rather than going from market to market buying things, it would be better if the concerned parties bought the things themselves [the gifts for the groom and his family and the dowry furniture]. *It would reduce our burden. . . . After the wedding, I learned that* [my future husband] *had given only 3,000,000 wôn to my mother-in-law and had pocketed 500,000 wôn for himself. At first, I didn't realize this. I found it out about it three months after the wedding. It was money that my parents had put together from their farming. . . . Every bit of the wedding money was from the harvest and sale of peaches. The very money we'd taken in, only just the day before, was bundled into that 3,500,000 wôn.*

Even with the stolen 500,000 wôn, this was a modest sum of marriage money at the time of her wedding (in 1982). I asked if she had worked before her marriage, knowing from other interviews that women who had not been able to save at least some of their earnings toward their weddings were often disadvantaged in marriage negotiations. After graduating from a commercial high school, she had worked for two and a half years, but had been forced to quit and help out at home when her mother was disabled by illness. Like many other working women with younger siblings, she had contributed her early wages to their education.

She answers my questions and takes up the thread of her story. A week after her marriage, her in-laws moved the couple from their own home into a room secured with a deposit of key money, and then the full truth of her situation was revealed.

. . . And then from the very next day, he came home drunk every night. Before even a month had passed, he insisted that we sell my gold double ring [a betrothal gift] *because he needed the money. I refused, but he insisted. I couldn't do anything about it. My ring was sold and the money spent. I might have held out, but I gave it to him to sell. I wondered what sort of person he was. They had said he had a job, but now it seemed that he did not. He had a lot of debts from when he had been single. He had used the 500,000 wôn of my wedding money and even the money from the sale of my gold ring to pay back debts. He was in debt because when he was single, not only had he been idle, but from eight months before our wedding, he had taken to smoking marijuana (taemach'o).*

At first, I didn't know what it was, but because my husband was acting so strangely, I began to be suspicious. There was something he always carried in his pocket. I confirmed my suspicions at the pharmacy. They told me it was marijuana. When I reported this fact to my in-laws, they called it a disaster. I don't think my in-laws had been totally ignorant up to that point. I think that while they knew, they denied it, so that when I told them, they behaved like people with split personalities.

We had been married for two months when I first mentioned it. We didn't even have marital relations. I asked a doctor in the clinic if someone who takes marijuana has trouble with his sexual performance. The doctor said that this was so. He said that someone who takes marijuana doesn't have any sex life, but even without sex, he is in such good spirits, so happy with himself that he doesn't need a wife.

This does not sound like marijuana to me; it sounds more like heroin. "Do you mean *hap'i sûmok* ('happy smoke')?" I ask, drawing from the depths of memory the word for "pot" that was current in the early 1970s.

"No," says Misuk, "*Apyôn*," opium. Perhaps she means "hard drugs."

He was also in debt because when he was a bachelor, his mother would abuse him for not having a job. She would only toss him a few coins. He borrowed money from his friends and got deeply into debt. That kind of life can't last. Since they had all turned marriageable age, they tallied up the debt and said, "Here's what you owe." . . . "If his home hadn't been so far away, we would have brought everything with us. We would not have entrusted the money to him, and he would not have had that windfall from it. . . ."

She puts the baby on her back, assisted by Misuk's mother as she bundles the baby's quilted carrying cloth around her body and secures the ties.

Until I learned from the doctor that he couldn't have any sex life, I automatically assumed that he disliked me. I brooded over the possibility that I had done something wrong. It would have been better for me if he had told me what was going on, but he kept it all a deep secret. . . . I went through so much mental anguish because I didn't know and thought that it was my fault. If he had talked to me, then it would have been tolerable, but apart from his demands, he said not a word. Take his clothes to the laundry, pick up the laundry, give him his laundered clothes, something to eat, money, this was the scope of his conversation. I was under a lot of mental stress. Although I had my family, they were far away and I couldn't talk to them. We didn't even have a telephone. It was still difficult for me to say anything to my in-laws. I couldn't tell them. I was frustrated. . . .

Although he had sold my gold ring after barely two months of marriage, I tried to be tolerant. Although he had gotten into debt when he was a bachelor, I said that since I was married to him, this outstanding debt should be repaid. Of course I was distressed and unhappy, but I thought that if we repaid the debt and he became more stable, then all would be well. But it was not to be. He spent everything on his own amusement and then, when there wasn't any money, he would badger me to death. At first, he had thought that since my family was living comfortably, he could tell me to ask them for money. According to the feudalistic customs of the countryside, divorce was considered a great blemish, so he calculated that country parents would give anything to prevent a divorce. He thought that he could harass me into going to my family for money, but I said, "Why should I?" When I held out, he began to abuse me more violently. He was mentally disturbed. To have a pleasant disposition, he had to take that stuff constantly. If he wasn't taking it, his chest would heave and he would get into a state and seem on the verge of doing himself some serious injury. When he couldn't take that stuff, he would drink himself senseless. He couldn't even walk by himself, he would sway on his feet. . . .

And his mind was twisted. He had sex with me once or twice in order to make me pregnant so that in other people's eyes, there wouldn't be anything amiss. If he didn't have a child, other people would consider him defective, but if he had a child, they would treat him like a normal person and not consider him strange. This way, I was the only one who would suffer.

She turns toward Misuk and her mother. "Am I leaving anything out?" Misuk, thoroughly familiar with her story, says, "Tell her how he came home late."

. . . *Even though he didn't have a job, he would go out when other people went to work and come back home at two or three in the morning. Even then, I would have to fix food for him. Whenever he came home, I was required to give him something to eat. . . . I thought that it was reasonable for me to feed him, I fed him without giving it any thought. A person has to eat to live. . . . He would demand food so I would always fix it. But he would be sleepy and doze off right in the middle of eating. Sometimes, he would be so full of liquor that he would fall dead asleep with the spoon falling out of his mouth. He was so drunk that sometimes he would piss right there inside the room. But no matter how late he went to sleep, at six a.m. sharp, he would get up, wash his face in cold water, groom himself, dress, and go out. If he came back in a good mood, I'd fix his food and he would eat it and go to sleep. But if he wasn't in a good mood, he would pick a fight with me while I was lying down, even if there was no reason to quarrel. . . .*

When we were first married . . . we lived near my husband's parents. With the dawn, I would go to my in-laws' house and work all day. When my mother-in-law came back at eight o'clock, I would go home and work. As soon as it was light, I would go back to my in-laws' house, and at the end of the day, come back to our house. This was also difficult. To suddenly be married and to find one's life totally changed took a lot of effort. But from my mother-in-law's point of view, what sort of effort did it take to do housework? . . . And in addition to that, my husband was behaving so strangely. I was terribly isolated. My mind was muddled. I couldn't grab hold of things. If you're wondering what sustained me, there was nothing. I was weighted down as I went about my tasks.

When I was seven months pregnant, my brother-in-law got married and I got a sister-in-law. . . . Because the second brother got along well with his family, they asked him to come and live with them. This was also so that the daughter-in-law would learn the family ways. . . . This was my good fortune. I didn't have to go over there every day, so things were easier. I was pregnant, of course, and everything had been so difficult I could have died. By the time my sister-in-law came to live with my husband's parents, I didn't have any strength left.

Although I had been very reliable at my work, I now felt relieved in the inner recesses of my heart. My sister-in-law was from Seoul, so things, like her method for making side dishes, weren't very different from theirs and didn't take so much effort. The food is very different in Pusan and Seoul, and it was hard for me to fix the side dishes the way the family liked them. . . . Even though I worked without pay, it would have been less exhausting if they had shown some appreciation for my effort. I was worn out in spirit. I thought that I would die. On top of that, my head and my back began to ache. When I recovered from the birth of my first child, I had lost ten pounds.

After my marriage, my husband would sometimes beat me very brutally. Beatings were a specialty with us. Once he got started, he wouldn't stop until he was just short of killing me. I'll tell you why he beat me for the first time. . . . Because my husband hadn't made any effort, in all his twenty-eight years he had never owned a trench coat. His brother-in-law let him wear his. My husband packed it up and took it away. Even after his wedding [when the bride's side gave him clothing], he didn't give the coat back to his sister. My husband's sister was pregnant, her belly was big at the time of our marriage. She came over and asked me, the newlywed, for the trench coat. She said, "My husband only intended for him to wear it, but he packed it up and took it away. Now that he's married, he must have a coat of his own. Why must he keep that one?"

I didn't understand her. She was telling me that we were keeping one of her husband's possessions in our home. When she said, "Sister-in-law, I'm going to take it back," I was so dumbfounded that she had to repeat herself.

When my husband came back at three in the morning I told him, "Your eldest sister came for the coat. She said that it was her husband's so I let her take it." He blew up because I had given it away without consulting him. Of course I was at fault for not consulting him, but she had said that she was taking her own husband's coat. What could I do about it? A husband is the person who lives with you. He should have at least instructed me as to what I could and could not give back and what I ought to know about each of his siblings.

He disregarded my baby. [She was newly pregnant.] *All he cared about was that I had given something away while he was out of the house. He grabbed hold of me and nearly tore my cheeks off. Because I was pregnant, I crouched over to protect my stomach* [she pantomimed it], *so instead, he concentrated on striking my face and biting at my back. My nose was bleeding. I opened the door to run out, but thinking that I would start screaming once I got outside, he grabbed me around the throat and I blacked out instantly.*

When I came to, I saw that there were identical cuts on both of my hands. I didn't know what they were, but then I saw that he was smeared red with blood. When I examined my wounds I could see that there were tooth marks where he had bitten me. He was so inhuman as to have sucked my blood.

In an instant, my husband turned his face away. While he had even sucked my blood, now he washed himself and went to sleep as if nothing had happened. The next day, when I saw the blood smeared all over, I got scared and without saying a word, went to get a medical report.

[She failed to certify her condition because the first hospital lacked an outpatient clinic and the second required an official document, probably a copy of the household register that would verify her marriage.]

I thought, "This is only the first time that I've been beaten. If I don't survive, then that's the end of it. What can I do if they refuse to give me medical certification?". . . I went back home. Before going to the hospital, I had called my in-laws to say I wouldn't be going over there that day. I was at the hospital when the third son and my mother-in-law came over. When they saw all the blood from my bloody nose and from where he bit me, they thought that I'd had a miscarriage. They knew that I was pregnant, but when they asked if I'd lost the baby, my husband blew up again . . . and screamed at them to leave.

[The couple continued to quarrel and when she threatened to get a divorce he beat her, and in a final burst of temper, threw his ashtray at her head.] *I took a fierce blow. My head began to hurt so much that it drove me crazy. At my in-laws' house, they gave me money for an x-ray and told my husband to go with me. We went to a neurology clinic for an examination. The doctor told my husband to wait outside and had me tell him everything about my life. He said that I had a nervous condition (singyông sông). The doctor called my husband back in and told him, "Your wife is on the verge of a nervous breakdown. Is there something wrong at home?"*

My husband, speaking earnestly, promised that he would not cause his wife nervous stress, that he would be more considerate in the future. I had brought the money for an x-ray, and . . . the doctor made the arrangements. But once we were outside, my husband said that we would forget about the x-ray. We would just get the medicine, take a taxi, and have lunch at a nice restaurant. It wasn't far and we could just as easily have eaten at home. I wanted to take the bus and put the money toward our living expenses. I wasn't able to have the x-ray that I wanted, that I had been told to get. Instead, he would take a taxi and have a nice lunch. What a warped person he is!

She describes how her husband cares only for his own appearance, buying brand name clothes and shoes on installment, although he has not held a job for longer than six months. "If you looked at him, you wouldn't think that anything was wrong." She, however, is not allowed to buy her own clothing and can never go out for lack of anything appropriate to wear. She speaks of how they live on the irregular payments and provisions doled out by her in-laws. She cannot even buy her own spices and condiments. She begins a rambling discussion of why she cannot divorce her husband and why she cannot go on living with him, the excruciating contradiction at the center of her existence. I write in my fieldnotes that by now, her eyes are very red.

Although I said that I would divorce, my parents could not accept it. . . . They firmly believe that, it wouldn't be right to have such a rumor arise [regarding one of their own children]. Since I do not want to injure my parents, I live with this weight pressing down on me, but I can't go on living this way for the rest of my life. I'm always ill at ease, thinking I'm going to be beaten to death, thinking that everything is ruined. There are new people living on both sides of our rented room so he can't do anything rash . . . but when we're by ourselves he'll insult me and strike me at will. I'm always tense. . . .

I could blame the granny who made my match, but she thought that he was a tranquil person. It wasn't as though she lied to me. She thought that since my mother-in-law was such a good person, her son must also be a good person. . . . It was my in-laws who lied so thoroughly to her. . . . They thought that if they married him off, then all would be well, but it hadn't worked that way, and I was the one who suffered the consequences. It's their fault. Therefore, so long as I live with their son, they help us out, cover our expenses, but they say that if I leave and get divorced, they won't give me even one wôn as compensation. . . .

Because her parents-in-law had so clearly wronged her in "playing the daughter-in-law for a fool," her own mother had tried to negotiate a compromise where the in-laws would set her up in business. Her husband's sister had denounced the plan as unrealistic for a woman with two small children, a waste of money on a venture that would surely fail. As she reviews her lack of options, her overwhelming sense of entrapment, she begins to cry in earnest.

In secret, I went a couple of times to the family court and asked for a divorce but they would not give me one because I lacked sufficient grounds. [Her husband had not abandoned her and there was no evidence of adultery.] *I'm growing old without anything to show for it. I have a nervous disease, I have headaches and backaches every day.*

[Her husband's kin continue to pressure her because her husband, as the eldest son, should have a male heir.] *I'm not a baby-making machine. . . . Leave aside the fact that my husband is sexually defective; if I were to have more children in my present state, it would kill me. My parents-in-law say they understand, but they don't know. They keep saying, "Have two more children.". . . When I think of my husband's temper, I want to disappear completely, right now, even if it means my own funeral. But for the present, this is my life. . . . A divorce is the only thing I'm capable of doing. If not that, then I have to make money if I am going to raise my children. But if I raise my children, I can't make money. Once or twice. . . I've thought of running away, but I don't have any savings, I don't have anything to take with me. I'm not able to escape. When I think of my parents, when I feel for them in my heart, then I endure.*

[She explains that she has no assets. Even her dowry furniture is stored in her in-laws' home. Only a few days before our meeting, she had pawned a gold ring, the last of her betrothal jewelry.] *Whenever I saw the ring on my finger, I felt a sense of satisfaction, I'd look at it and feel courage, a will to go on. . . . My mother is always telling me that I must take what comes. When I'm heavy-hearted and I talk this way to my husband's maternal aunts, they tell my husband to treat me better, but that just drives him wild and makes him even more unbearable. . . . I think that it would be best for me to leave my two children behind and sneak away, but I don't have anywhere to go, and because of my children, I can't go. He doesn't abuse me so badly in the daytime but as soon as it's night, he gets into a state, intimidates me with a knife or some such, and then the next day, he's better. . . .*

If only he didn't always say that he despised me and didn't bully me. Even though he's no husband to me, I've known him for a long time and could get by happily with such scraps of conversation as "Hey, I want to eat meat," or "Buy me some cigarettes." We could go on living, and if we didn't have money, we could borrow and get by. . . .

She is sobbing now. I fumble in my bag for a tissue and hand it to her. Misuk's mother's eyes are filled with tears. The backs of my eyelids sting. She isn't an interview subject from whom I can easily walk away. I want to help her, but what can I do? Lamely, I fumble in my bag again, looking for the card of a counseling service specializing in family problems, a reform-oriented organization that I have visited during my research. She glances at the card and nods helplessly. She has already been there several times. They have told her that she should divorce since she is a person who has no hope for a better marriage, but divorce would mean leaving her children. They would be well cared for by her in-laws but she would lose them. She says that she has seen programs on television where children resent the mother who left them and then tries to see them after years of absence.

I don't want to hurt my children. It would be different if I were to leave them behind and go out and make a lot of money, if I were to bring money back to them, go to America or some place, but that's not how things are.

In one breath, she says that she must wait for her divorce until her children are safely married. With the next, she acknowledged that her marriage is damaging her children. Ultimately, she admits, *"I can't even make money. I have a nervous condition and can't do the sort of work that would set it off. Though I may look healthy and not in pain, I'm a sick person and I have no hope for my life."*

Hiring a divorce lawyer would also take money, several hundred thousand wôn. It makes her head hurt to think of it. The counseling service has told her that her chances of getting compensation are slim since her husband has nothing and she lives apart from her in-laws. And then there is her loyalty to her own family, to her parents' values, and to her five unmarried siblings, whose prospects would be damaged by the blemish of her divorce.

She speaks of how, when her parents came for a visit, she had wanted to treat them well, but a day's cooking sent her to bed with flu-like aches and lethargy. The tasks that she is still expected to perform at her in-laws' house tax her with unbearable physical pain. *"I get stressed and then I have to lie down for days without any strength. When I think of it, I'm strange too."*

With only lay knowledge, I recognize the symptoms of acute depression. I also recognize the Korean idiom of acute bodily pain as a sign of profound mental suffering. I tell her that her illness is a consequence of her heavy-hearted (*taptaphada*) circumstances. She says that she has been told this before. I am not surprised.

She describes a dead end, but she can also imagine a path out. Her sister and brother-in-law have told her to get an automatic divorce by deserting the home for six months. They tell her that they will help to set her up in a shop, that she can remarry.

My sister and brother-in-law have been urging me to divorce from before I had even been married for a year, but I felt that what's done is done. The truth is I'm just living from day to day. I don't have any hope. . . . I would like to go somewhere far away, to a foreign country and live. It would be better if my family could move to another place where there wouldn't be any rumors, and then I could easily get divorced. But it isn't so easy to move.

She continues in this vein, thinking aloud. She cannot get divorced. She cannot bear to stay married. Her situation is intolerable. As an empathetic chorus, we affirm that she has been wronged and that she suffers. Guiltily, I realize that I am already late for an appointment in another part of the city. I don't know how to bring this interview to an end. It seems callous to signal closure by coughing, shifting in place, or packing up my tape recorder. She has given me the story of her pain, planted it in the notebook on my lap and in my tape recorder. What are her expectations of me? Does she entertain even a faint hope that I might find her a visa to a distant place? I have nothing more to offer her than a tissue to mop her eyes and the redundant telephone number of a counseling service. She continues to catalogue her dilemma.

I can't stop thinking that if we continue to live together, some day, when he's feeling his strength, he'll kill me. . . . If only he didn't beat me, then I wouldn't always be so ill at ease. I'm always on edge. . . . But whatever his condition, at six o'clock the next morning he gets right up, washes his face, and then, quick as a flash, he puts on the dress shirt I've ironed for him, the socks I've washed for him, the underpants I've washed for him, gets dressed and goes out. [This sequence has the rhythm of an incantation and is probably the product of many tellings.] *The women in the neighborhood think my husband cuts a good figure and think that he must do well by his wife. . . . It isn't easy to talk to them. . . . If I speak of my frustration they call me a crazy woman. . . .* [Even so, she exchanges confidences with a neighbor.] *" 'How can you go on living with that man? If it were me, I wouldn't put up with it. You've already said you're not going to put up with it. Why do you*

go on this way?' She calls me a fool. . . . It's easy for her to talk about
someone else's situation, but it's difficult for me to reach a decision."

Our encounter is one more replay of this conversation—
with a sympathetic listener and simultaneously with herself.
Many such conversations are implicit in her story: with her parents, her siblings, her husband's aunts, the neurology doctor, the
family counselors, the court, and sympathetic neighbors like
Misuk's mother. She speaks of lies and silences, of the respectable
facade that masked her husband's late-night brutality, of her own
isolation, her inability to speak, "even now." She cannot tell her
in-laws the truth about her husband's sexual failings. Her own
parents do not know the full details of her marriage. Her neighbors call her "crazy" for publicly criticizing her husband. And
the tale has burst out, even so. Misuk, her mother, and I with
my tape recorder are all privy to intimate details of her marital
relationship. The very act of telling and listening, and the
responses of those who hear her story, validate the utter impos-
sibility of her situation. She cannot divorce without painful consequences for herself, her children, her parents, and her brothers
and sisters. And yet she must divorce.

As I gather up my things and prepare to depart, I take her
hand in both of mine and wish her well. She is composed now,
her tears dry. She says that she does not like to tell her story over
and over again, weeping with each fresh telling. She says that she
only did it today because I am a foreigner. She is composed now.
Her tears are dry. She repeats Misuk's mother's insistence that I
stay to lunch and when I demure politely, she walks with us to
the gate. I feel shaken and very sad. On our way down the hillside, Misuk says to me, "I think that auntie is going to get
divorced." In a few days, Misuk will report that this is her young
neighbor's decision.

I understand then that despite her reluctance to tell her story
and weep, the telling was both a necessary act and a necessarily
repetitive act. Each telling, each confirmation from her listeners
that her marriage was truly intolerable moved her a hair's
breadth closer to divorce. Her clear and anecdotal account of

how her marriage came about, how she so willingly committed herself on the basis of very little information and in total ignorance of her husband's character, must have been polished by numerous recitations. The story of her first beating is similarly told with precision and logic of sequence. Once muddled, she has gained a clear-headed sense of her own victimization ("I thought that it was my fault."). Only when she has set it all out and begins to confront the underlying question—can she stay in such a marriage—only then do her words become disjointed as she rambles from argument to counterargument.

Her tale is a tale in motion, deployed in the hope of finding a way out of an impasse or of making peace with it. The italicized tale would not suffice without the context of its telling. But to include the context is also to acknowledge the American anthropologist and her tape recorder. I carried this unhappy woman's tale away with me, and it now sits as tape and transcript beside a bundle of cautions about the politics of such encounters.[3] It was my privileged position as a "foreigner," a professor, and Misuk's employer that had brought about our meeting. Did Misuk's neighbor have expectations of me? Did she think that I could find her a visa to America, where she could earn the money to redeem her children? All I had to offer her was a tissue and the redundant telephone number of a counseling service. Was I then going to capitalize upon her pain in the currency of academic production? Or can it be, as Aihwa Ong suggests, that "Given our privileges, there is greater betrayal in allowing our personal doubts to stand in the way of representing . . . [our subjects'] claims, interests, and perspectives. The greater betrayal lies in refusing to recognize informants as active cultural producers in their own right, whose voices insist on being heard and can make a difference in the way we think about their lives" (Ong 1995, 353–354).

It would be not only superficial but also wrong to read this tale as one more typification of victimized Korean womanhood. Certainly, she has been victimized and cries out against it: "I was the only one who would suffer." "I was the woman who suffered the consequences." Her tale is a painful illustration of structural and ideological limitations, of unrealistic family expectations, of an absence of legal protection,[4] of "the feudalistic customs of the countryside." But while her own mother counsels her to accept her lot and she herself states that "what's done is done," her actions, even to the telling of the tale, do not suggest passivity. With ironic detachment, she describes how her mother-in-law "thought that a countrywoman would be hard working and have a simple and honest disposition." This is not how she presents herself. In secret, she tried to get medical certification for her first beating. In secret, she has gone to the Family Court and to the counseling center. She has sought out confidants who will hear her grievances and has woven their judgments into subsequent tellings of her story, playing devil's advocate against their advice. The very act of telling, as a stumbling attempt to come to terms with her situation, of finding the resolve to end her marriage, is an act of agency.

Lila Abu-Lughod (1993) and Ruth Behar (1993), among others, have argued that we must listen carefully to women's own stories as a means of destabilizing the "ethnographic typifications" that render all subjects distant and strange and that commonly render "third world women" as passive, subservient, and lacking in creativity. Misuk's neighbor wants her listeners, both Korean and foreign, to understand the precise circumstances of her life, to understand them as outrageous and abnormal, as anything but "typical," and to understand why it is so difficult for her to take obvious advice. Even as she disassociates herself from "the feudalistic customs of the countryside," she must explain (and not just to me) why this antique ideology has the power to damage those she loves. Her story weaves in multiple points of view as she debates simultaneously with her listeners and with those who have listened before.

I might have left Misuk's neighbor's story in fragments, as the passing reference that appeared in my book on Korean weddings, "the story of an innocent country woman married to an urban ne'er-do-well through the machinations of his desperate mother. The bride became a battered wife who, at the time of our interview, was on the verge of filing for divorce" (Kendall 1996, 9). The tepid construction "was on the verge of filing for divorce" does not hint at Misuk's neighbor's own engagement with her situation. The reader would never imagine that the act of telling her story—the "interview" that engendered the "data"— was itself an assault upon the circumstances so blandly described in the published ethnography. I have learned a great deal from what she tried to tell me. This was a tale that willed itself to be retold.

NOTES

1. The notion that marriage will mature an unruly young man seems to be common (Kendall 1986, 8–10).
2. Houses are numbered by the sequence of their construction rather than by spatial sequence, and it is often difficult to locate a new address. Someone from the household will often meet visitors near a bus stop or subway station and guide them to the house.
3. Feminist ethnographers who write about women in non-Western settings now recognize that these encounters are never innocent of the distinctions of class, culture, and global operations of power in which both interviewer and subject participate. The ethnographer writes from a position of privilege, and "women" do not necessarily share a common consciousness. Critics contend that where a naive feminism assumes a universal condition of oppression for "third world women," it generalizes its subjects to the point of stereotype (Mohanty 1988; Trinh 1989). See other self-critical discussions of anthropological practice by Abu-Lughod (1990), Behar (1990, 1993), Gordon (1993), Ong (1988), Visweswaran (1994), and Wolf (1992), and from the perspective of sister disciplines by Spivak (1988), Stacey (1988), and the several contributors to the volume edited by Gluck and Patai (1991), among others.
4. Her "ethnographic present" is two years before the reform of the Family Law at the end of 1989. While it remains to be seen how substantial the reforms are in actual practice, women's limited recourse in divorce was the prime motivation of the reformers.

REFERENCES

Abu-Lughod, Lila. 1990. Can there be a feminist ethnography? *Women and Performance: A Journal of Feminist Theory* 5:25.

———. 1993. *Writing Women's Worlds: Bedouin Stories.* Berkeley: University of California Press.

Behar, Ruth. 1990. Rage and redemption: Reading the life story of a Mexican marketing woman. *Feminist Studies* 16(2):223–258.

———. 1993. *Translated Woman: Crossing the Border with Esperanza's Story.* Boston: Beacon Press.

Gluck, Sherna Berger, and Daphne Patai, eds. 1991. *Women's Words: The Feminist Practice of Oral History.* New York and London: Routledge.

Gordon, Deborah A. 1993. The unhappy relationship of feminism and postmodernism in anthropology. *Anthropological Quarterly* 66(3):109–117.

Grima, Benedicte. 1992. The role of suffering in women's performance of Paxto. In *Gender, Genre, and Power in South Asian Expressive Traditions,* edited by Arjun Appadurai et al., 78–101. Philadelphia: University of Pennsylvania Press.

Kendall, Laurel. 1988. *The Life and Hard Times of a Korean Shaman: Of Tales and the Telling of Tales.* Honolulu: University of Hawaii Press.

———. 1996. *Getting Married in Korea: Of Gender, Morality, and Modernity.* Berkeley: University of California Press.

Mohanty, Chandra. 1988. Under Western eyes: Feminist scholarship and colonial discourses. *Feminist Review* 30:61–88.

Ong, Aihwa. 1988. Colonialism and modernity: Feminist re-presentations of women in non-Western societies. *Inscriptions* 3(4):79–93.

———. 1995. Women out of China: Traveling tales and traveling theories in postcolonial feminism. In *Women Writing Culture,* edited by Ruth Behar and Deborah A. Gordon, 350–372. Berkeley: University of California Press.

Spivak, Gayatri Chakravorty. 1988. Can the subaltern speak? In *Marxism and the Interpretation of Culture,* edited by Nelson and Grossberg, 271–312. Urbana and Chicago: University of Illinois Press.

Stacey, Judith. 1988. Can there be a feminist ethnography? *Women's Studies International Forum* 11(1):21–27.

Trinh, T. Minh-ha. 1989. *Woman, Native, Other: Writing Postcoloniality and Feminism.* Bloomington: Indiana University Press.

Visweswaran, Kamala. 1994. *Fictions of Feminist Ethnography.* Minneapolis: University of Minnesota Press.

Wolf, Margery. 1992. *A Thrice Told Tale: Feminism, Postmodernism, and Ethnographic Responsibility.* Stanford, CA: Stanford University Press.

The Freak Street Riots of '59

DAVID HENDERSON

Nudging my way into the line of people circumambulating Ganesh's temple, I hear the clock tower across town begin its pleasingly discordant morning rendition of eight o'clock. I yawn; my worn-out knee seems to ache more with each peal of the bell. I'm really getting too old to be running my shop alone. I should hire someone young and ambitious to open in the mornings.

My visit to Ganesh complete, I head past the old royal palace. Once again my eyes make me look along its south face, down Old New Road. Once again my eyes stop and retrace their steps. And when they drag my attention back to what used to be called Freak Street, once again I fail to ignore memories of charred ruins and portentiously loud silences. Every morning, my silly head faithfully restores these fragments of the past on the freshly swept brick plaza to the south of the palace. Every day, remembered images come to me like familiar faces emerging from a crowd.

Heading past the row of shops along the west flank of the palace, I hear the plaintive cries of the Asian Dub Foundation screeching out of the speakers in my younger brother's shop.

Like many other young punks around the city, my brother Dinesh is really nostalgic about the fifties—I mean the 2050s, according to our Bikram Sambat (the late '90s, in the A.D. system). I don't know what that era holds for him. I remember him as a clean-cut boy dressed in a light blue shirt and dark blue pants running carelessly off to school. He looked a miniature Nepali traffic cop and exuded that same sense of control over his small world—a sense of control that was entirely negated by the swirling chaos that surrounded him. And I was a part of that chaos. I believed in rock and roll back then.

I don't see anyone amid the many-colored masks in Dinesh's shop, but Hari Prasad, who owns the *thanka* shop next door, sees me from behind his patchwork display of mandala paintings and yells out that my brother is looking for me, that he has a customer for me. I nod my head in thanks and walk over to his shop to linger a moment and fulfill a daily ritual I have with him. First, I am required to needle him about not yet being married, as he's in his early thirties. I remark today that the noise of Dinesh's stereo must be scaring all Hari Prasad's marriage prospects away. In response, he usually says something about my being well on my way to biting my tongue—if you'd ever been to the meat market down by the river and seen all the severed goats' heads leering at you, tongues protruding between clenched teeth, you'd understand this euphemism for death. This morning, though, Hari Prasad replies only that the music keeps the ghosts away, that he has prospects all over the city, that the loud music of my youth did nothing to keep my wife away. Laughing, I am obliged to agree and continue on my way, past Hanuman, past Kali Bhairab, and past the north edge of the old palace grounds. My shop is in an upstairs room on the narrow road that cuts diagonally toward Indrachok, and, as I climb the steps, I see Dinesh and a tanned, backpacked, probably European man, standing there waiting for me. As I turn my key in the oversized padlock on the door to my shop, my brother scolds me for opening late and chides me for being lazy. I know he's joking. But I wish my body was still full of the energy that seems to possess him.

Inside, I pull out a few stools for Dinesh and the foreigner. The man seems travel worn, but his eyes bespeak a childlike curiosity. I've seen these crazy blue eyes in many tourists. But I've also seen, in tourists who have become long-term friends and return occasionally to Kathmandu, that the wild hue in their eyes fades to a wiser shade of pale blue. Dinesh introduces the man as Mister Werner. He's always very polite to foreigners; I used to be, but I dropped my stilted and awkward use of formalities long ago.

I hear the tea boy downstairs and yell for him to bring three glasses of tea. Apologizing to Werner for being late, I ask for his patience as I light three sticks of sandalwood incense. I begin a brief prayer in front of Laxmi, whose small shrine sits in a corner of my shop, then take the incense to the door of my shop and make three circles in the air. Meanwhile, Dinesh begins our usual ritual with tourists, asking Werner how he likes Nepal, how long he'll be staying, what he'll be doing here. Part of this ritual is simply to make ourselves appear friendly and interested in our customers; part of it is to feel out their plans in the hopes of generating business for friends of ours who run trekking and tour offices on the street below.

I wedge the burning incense into a crack in the concrete floor in front of the shrine. Taking a few flower petals from my shirt pocket, I place one on Werner's head and several on Dinesh's head, placing my palms together in front of my face and bowing slightly to each of them in turn. I then place a few petals on my own head and finish my words to Laxmi. Grabbing a short broom from near the door, I squat to sweep out the entrance to my shop. I'm just finishing as the tea boy brings our tea. I give him a few worn hundred-rupee notes, pass glasses of tea to my guests, and take a loud sip of mine as I settle onto a stool. Now I'm ready for business.

I ask Werner if he is interested in one of the many Tibetan carpets I have on display in my shop, or perhaps if he is looking instead for some of my carved rosewood boxes. He replies, in his German-tinted English, that he is actually there to offer something to me. Although I tell him that I'm not interested in purchasing anything, he insists on at least showing me what is in his backpack. He explains.

"Early this morning I am valking to the Omniscient Monkey to have a coffee, ja? Und a little boy comes down ze street kicking a ball. Oder I should say zat I belief it is a ball zen. He gets close und I see zis ball besser. It is a curious artifact, zis thing. I give him thousand rupees for it, ja? He is happy und runs off into a courtyard to show his mutter, I think. I put ze artifact in my rucksack, und after drinking coffee I take it to your brudder's mask shop und show it to him. Und he says he has nicht seen such thing before, und bringen me here."

Setting his tea down, he reaches into his backpack and pulls out a large round object wrapped in a dirty pink towel, placing it on the floor in front of me. He carefully removes the towel. The bruised and muddied plastic head of Ronald McDonald grins up at me.

This is not the first time Ronald has looked at me in this way. This time, though, his glazed gaze summons forth all my memories of the events of '59. It's been years since I've told anyone this story, but something about Werner's cheerful innocence makes me want to tell it to him. Dinesh has heard it all before, and he finishes his tea and scoots apologetically out the door back to his shop. Werner's crazy blue eyes watch him go, and he looks momentarily uncomfortable. I ask him politely if he has time to listen to this story. Foreigners never seem to have time here to engage in the long hours of gossip I enjoy. They're always jangling madly up and down the street, as if the moment they wish to inhabit is always somewhere ahead of the crush of honking taxis and bell-ringing rickshaws.

Werner relaxes a bit and shrugs his shoulders as if to suggest I should go ahead and tell my tale. Now, my English isn't so good. I studied a bit in school. I memorized pages and pages of song lyrics by the Eagles, the Doors, and Metallica. But during the last twenty years or so, my English has been confined to these brief encounters with tourists. I can tell many things about carpet-making and woodcarving in perfect English, but other subjects find me struggling for words. So I was only able to tell him bits and pieces of this story. Had I the words, this is what I would have told.

* * *

It was the month of Bhadra in '59. I think that would be August of 2002 according to your calendar—near the time of *gai jatra,* when all those crazy parody songs and comic books start hitting the market. I had decided that if I was going to be on the billing with Ricky Martin and the Backstreet Boys at the grand opening of the new Wal-Mart store, I first ought to have a look inside this great emporium of the West. So there I was, sliding around on the waxed floors, not knowing for sure whether I felt nauseous or euphoric. Anxious for a breath of fresh air amid the seemingly endless shelves of lightly scented products, I escaped from an aisle and wandered into a forest of women's clothes. A neon-lit clearing beckoned to me, and, emerging from a dense underbrush of lingerie, I was welcomed by the hardened grin of Ronald McDonald. Ronald was made of a particularly fine grade of molded plastic. He was sitting on one end of a displaced park bench, with one leg swung nonchalantly over the other, beckoning shoppers into this billions-and-billions-sold paradise gently crammed into a corner of the store. I perched lightly on his knee, needing a moment to sort through remembered scraps of newspaper articles. It was inevitable that Wal-Mart would have brought its particular brand of generica to this side of the world. But I thought they were going to put it somewhere north of Ring Road, on the outskirts of town. I was shocked to find instead that the souvenir hawkers at the end of Freak Street had been swept from the street to make way for Wal-Mart Kathmandu, the flagship South Asian store fabricated in Arkansas and deposited like a gleaming white turd amidst the brown facades and golden roofs of Durbar Square.

Why here? Why now, as wayward missiles aimed from India to Pakistan floated lazily overhead to their demise on the slopes of the Himalayas? Only a few years earlier college students had thwarted Tipper Gore's official visit by firebombing the library of the United States Information Service, sending shock waves across fax lines to Washington, D.C., and forcing the cancellation of her trip. And last year someone had smuggled a live tiger into Ambassador George W. Bush, Jr.'s Fourth of July celebrity bash. Boris, the resident feline at the Yak and Yeti Hotel, had found herself suddenly free to investigate the exotic aroma of barbecue. Red McCombs, a Texas car dealer turned football-team owner, was in the midst of a goodwill speech when Boris sauntered through the gate to the ambassador's house. Unfortunately, Red was standing directly in front of the barbecue, and just as he was about to pledge a gift of 300 Suburbans to the government of Nepal, Boris attacked him instead of the ribs. She managed to tear out his galvanized larynx before two of the guests from the Minnesota Vikings wrestled her to the ground, where a fresh U.S. Marine pumped 27 slugs into her body. The United Marxist-Leninists claimed credit for the tiger's emancipation. So did a previously unknown Tibetan terrorist group calling themselves the Abominable Yellow Snowmen. The *Kathmandu Post* had been quick to wish Red a speedy recovery, yet didn't fail to mention that the Suburbans had been outlawed recently in the United States as the result of new emissions regulations. The taxidermist meanwhile had his work cut out for him trying to patch the bullet holes in Ambassador Bush's new rug.

In any case, I had returned to Nepal only recently from a trip to the United States. Wal-Mart was using me to promote their new sense of global awareness—which wasn't entirely convincing, despite an expensive advertising campaign that featured a computer-generated image of Wal-Mart founder Sam Walton proudly calling his store the "international hometown store." So to boost their image among younger shoppers who liked to think of themselves as globally responsible citizens,

Wal-Mart had sponsored my appearance at the annual South By Southwest music festival in Austin, Texas. While I was there, they also made sure that I had the opportunity to visit some of their stores, as well as their visitor's center in Arkansas. Now, back in Kathmandu, I recognized subtle differences between this store and the ones I had seen in Round Rock, Taylor, and other towns on the road to Bentonville, Arkansas. For instance, I first noticed a light mist as I walked in the door; the cheerful septuagenarian Wal-Mart People Greeter stationed there explained to me in friendly tones that it contained antibacterial ingredients. Also, I found that a religious paraphernalia section had been added, including items such as incense, vermilion powder, stick-on *tikas,* dashboard Shivas, and small plastic Buddhas ("Made With Pride in the USA," proclaimed the packaging vainly). And although I didn't find any Nepali cassettes hiding in the midst of the pop, rock, country, and Latin music sections, I did encounter a few stray cassettes of Chinese and Vietnamese pop songs.

Still, though, that eerie sense of sameness pervaded the store. Large bags of potato chips still sold for about two dollars, or two hundred rupees. Several different sizes and brands of automatic coffeemakers jammed the shelves, eager to change the ways of the inhabitants of this tea-drinking land. And hundreds of bottles of Pert were arranged in tidy rows like barrel-chested green soldiers making a frontal attack on Nepali hygiene.

The bass player in my band, Indra, drifted lazily out of a hanging cloud of gray sweatshirts. He said furtively that he had been looking for me, that we needed to talk, and pulled me by the arm into the restaurant. After grudgingly buying him a buff burger and getting a lychee pie and some fries for myself, we settled into a booth near an Indian family and their overfed shopping cart. A Jimmy Buffett song filtered out of the ceiling somewhere. I hummed along impassively as I looked around for a salt shaker.

Chewing a bite of burger, Indra began talking in a quiet monotone. "The Maoists came to my house last night. They want to do something at the store at the grand opening, and they need our help. I didn't know what to say, but then they told me that they would kill my father if we didn't help."

Now, Indra's father is an old, old man. He remembers what Kathmandu was like before the Nepali Congress Party-led government began its overhaul of the tourism industry. He even remembers what Kathmandu was like before the massive industrialization of the '30s. About all he ever does is sit around remembering things. On sunny days he often dozes on a grass mat on the roof of Indra's house, but I'm sure that even his dreams have been deeply scored and grooved by the continuous recycling of antiquated memories. Why the Maoists would threaten his life was beyond me, but I never could make sense of some of their tactics.

* * *

While I am telling this story, my friend Christine comes into the shop. I pull out a stool for her and call for some more glasses of tea. Christine is an anthropologist from Bali; she's doing some sort of project down in Patan, just across the river from Kathmandu, at some of the Hindu temples there. I know her because she's a pretty good chess player and drops by on occasion for a game or two. She has heard this story before, but I don't think she understood much of it when I first told it to her.

Touching a button on her Sony, she begins recording my tale. We've talked about this already; I don't understand why she wants to record all this useless talk. I've told her that it's a waste of her batteries, but she can do what she wants. It's not like it makes me nervous or anything. I used to be in front of the microphone all the time.

* * *

"Margaritaville" spun to a close, and I glanced at the Indian family as I waited for another song to come on and mask our voices from them. Clearly, they were too involved in the antics of their young son to notice us anyway. The boy was defiantly throwing McNuggets at his father, who was quietly but threateningly telling him to stop.

As Anjali Pepper's recent medley of "Made in India" and "Born in the U.S.A." started grinding out of the ceiling speakers, I leaned over my fries and spoke to Indra. "Listen. You know that I've been critical of this whole Wal-Mart deal all along. When I agreed to put my musical abilities to work for those NGO liars in the '40s, I never anticipated that this was what they meant by 'development.' "

I paused to chew a bite of pie and chew my thoughts one last time, then swallowed and continued. "You know my father has been fighting against just this kind of meddling for many years now. And maybe you know that I'm starting to give up on this rock thing. I thought I could change things. I thought I would do for Nepal what Cui Jian has done for China or Rhoma Irama has done for Indonesia." I was pretty naive back then, you understand. "But maybe now is the time to be activists, using grenades rather than guitars to argue our ideas. As long as they're planning a clean strike, I'll help."

Indra gobbled down the last of his burger. "Good. We're supposed to meet someone at the French Cultural Centre on Saturday afternoon at two. They're showing an old Cocteau film. You know nobody ever goes to those film screenings, and everyone will be home watching the Hindi matinee on Nepal TV anyway. The cinema hall should be the most private place to discuss their plans and our involvement."

He stood up to leave and shook my hand in parting. Not his usual style. Looking disgustedly at the Indian boy, who was adorning his nostrils with his fries, Indra shuffled out of the restaurant and vanished into a thicket of garments. "Ke garne?" I asked myself. What can I do? I don't know that I've ever been able to come to a decision freely. The choice Indra gave me had already been made.

* * *

More tea glasses arrive, and I take a moment to introduce Christine to Werner and ask Christine where she's been, where she's going today. She apologizes to Werner for diverging into Nepali: "I sometime forget how to speak the English, yes? Sorry. Maaf garnus, hai ta?" she says, with a smile I swear she learned in Nepal.

She kills her Sony, then turns to me and continues. "You know that big Laxmi temple down on the south end of Patan? That one you took me to on Saturday?"

I wag my head in assent.

"The whole courtyard is now filled with slot machines. There's no space left for worship. I asked my friend Banuji about it, and she said the Clean Green Lalitpur Organization put the slot machines in to raise money for a fleet of electric rickshaws for the city. But I thought the mayor had promised that temples and the courtyards surrounding them would remain off limits to development projects."

"Eh, Christine *baini,*" I reply. "You didn't see the news last night, did you? The prime minister declared that the government would now officially sanction the use of slot machines at Laxmi temples. You remember when I won a thousand rupees playing chess last year around Laxmi Puja? Gambling is a form of worship where Laxmi Devi is concerned. With his announcement, the prime minister simply acknowledged that the *naya yuga*—the New Age—is here to stay, and the government wants to eat a piece of it."

Christine scoffs. "I don't know about this New Age stuff. I heard about something like this in America back in the '30s. All these people so obsessed with their own enlightenment that they forgot to pay attention to anything else. Slot machines cut people off from devotional expression, from social interaction, don't they? People get absorbed in the clank-clanking of rupees and the spinning of religious icons on the slot wheels, and it seems like they are distancing themselves from Laxmi rather than drawing near to her."

"I don't know, *baini*. There's not much difference between slot wheels and prayer wheels. And if we're going to make our Hindu path more profitable in the tourist industry, we must make it easier to understand. Nobody's going to come to Nepal to experience confusion. We must give them a taste of enlightenment."

"Yes, but does Laxmi really want the worship of tourists?" retorts Christine. "Anyway, my feeling is that the slot machines are going to eat the money of Nepalis, not tourists. We'll see. I had hoped that the government would have kept all this conversion of culture into capital confined to Swayambhu City. But now social practices are becoming just like those cheap old cassettes you were telling me about, recorded on ribbons of magnetized plastic and encased in plastic shells. I don't know. I've always wondered what it was like back in Sapir's day, back when people talked about culture as if it was a way of life."

Christine often seems to get nostalgic for things I don't quite understand. "People are people," I tell her. "Why shouldn't tourists have the chance to buy another way of life if they're discontent with what their civilization has given them?"

"Yeah, I suppose you're right," shrugs Christine. "I suppose people will treat ways of life—even those that they purchase—as if they were more like digital sound files, sampling, distorting, and remixing them to suit their needs. But whatever culture is, it's supposed to be a good thing, right?"

"I don't know, *baini*. I don't know."

We finish our tea in silence. Christine looks at Werner, who is leaning on the windowsill watching the traffic below. She says to him, in English, "Sorry to interrupt Mahesh's story. Please, you come and hear more." Werner pulls himself back inside. Christine touches the button on her Sony as if to cue me to resume my story.

* * *

So that Friday night we had a rehearsal on the roof of the Hotel Mount Fuji in Thamel, a few minutes north of here. The big Wal-Mart opening was planned for Sunday, and we had invited all our friends to hang out and drink *sake* while we ran through our numbers. Many people showed up—mostly Nepali men in their twenties, but a few of the Japanese women who were staying at the hotel wandered up to see what all the noise was about. I did a cover of a Pizzicato Five song for them, but for the most part we stuck to the set we would use at the Wal-Mart concert. You know, stuff by the Eagles and the Doors, some Jimi Hendrix songs, and a few songs of our own. Oh, yeah—since we were opening for Ricky Martin, we also worked up a reggae version of an old Menudo song, "Parque del oeste," which we were doing as "Parque del este." It was a good rehearsal, but as usual the police came and shut us up well before midnight. We hung out, drinking *sake,* for a few hours with the other hotel "managers"—that was what we liked to call ourselves, although mostly what we did during the day was sit around the lobby, smoking cigarettes, strumming guitars, and waiting for business. With the emptying of the last bottle, we poured ourselves down the stairs to sleep and speculate on the events of the next two days.

The next afternoon, after we had doused ourselves liberally in cups of tea and instant coffee, we walked over to the French Cultural Centre. The cinema hall was dark when we went in, and the film was just starting—Cocteau's *La belle et la bête.* As our eyes adjusted to the dark, we saw that the four of us—Indra and myself, plus our drummer and guitar player—were alone in the hall. Indra and I used to go there when we were younger, expecting to meet some nice French women. But that never happened. All the nice French women, and probably the not-so-nice ones as well, were probably hanging out in the Thamel bars hoping to meet some nice Nepali men.

About ten or fifteen minutes into the film, a Nepali couple came in and sat down behind us. The man began firing soft but firm Newari words at me. They hit my ears like rubber bullets at first. But I relaxed when it became apparent that our involvement in this Maoist plot was going to be minimal. They wanted us to create a distraction just as the clock tower began striking five o'clock and suggested that we rig an amplifier with an explosive device, which they would provide, to start a small electrical fire. The woman explained that the main action would be happening in the store itself; we were to play on a small stage to the side of the store, so would be far away from the real trouble. Expressing my assent, I heard a rustling sound behind me, then felt something shove up against my feet. The couple became quiet for a time. After about ten minutes, they got up to leave. The woman, who smelled of French perfume, leaned down and said something in Indra's ear. The man, who reeked of Chinese brandy, told me to pick up the package at my feet when I left.

All those afternoons spent in the Centre waiting for French women who never materialized at least had cultivated a taste for those wild old films of Cocteau's, and we stayed for the entire showing. I had seen this one before with a gentle old Jesuit priest whom I knew, who had explained the plot in Nepali as we watched. Toward the end of the film, La Belle's suitor and her brother head off into the forest to steal the riches from the temple of Diana at La Bête's castle. The two of them climb the wall of the temple and peer down through the skylight at the wealth strewn below. The suitor breaks the skylight and asks the brother to lower him into the temple. But as he dangles in the air, the statue of Diana comes to life and shoots an arrow through his back. Horrified, La Belle's brother lets go of the suitor, and he plunges to the floor, where, as he lies broken and bleeding, his body transforms into that of La Bête. I couldn't help thinking of the package at my feet as the arrow of Diana, which tomorrow we would aim at the heart of old Sam Walton down by Freak Street.

As the projector clicked to a halt, I picked up the package and slid it gingerly into my leather jacket, then trailed my band out into the hazy afternoon sun. We tried to stroll nonchalantly back to the hotel, but there was nothing nonchalant about the lump next to my heart. Back at the hotel, we unwrapped the package and found a remote detonator and a small bomb wrapped in newspaper. Written on the page was a brief note in blunt and shaky Nepali, giving directions for using the bomb and concluding with a reminder of the threat to Indra's father. I burned the note, put the devices in a plastic bag, stuffed them into my guitar case, and slid it under my bed. We trotted over to the Blue Note for a few beers, eager to blot out our reckless imaginings of what would take place the next day.

* * *

Just then a young bearded Japanese head appears in the doorway. The rest of a man follows. Shyly, he says, "Maaf garnus. I am interrupting."

Christine interrupts him. "That's okay. He was speaking a story to us. It can wait a moment. Can we help you?" She turns off her Sony.

"I am looking for National Museum." He holds out a tattered guidebook for Christine's inspection. "My book show it near Swayambhu, but I am not finding it. The man downstair not knowing. He say you up here maybe knowing."

Flipping back to the beginning of the book, Christine looks at it a moment and exclaims, "Copyright 1987? There's your problem, honey. The National Museum is no more. The building is there, yes. But ten years ago, the Soaltee Oberoi took it over, and, with the help of the government, began turning it into this Shangri-La-La-Land. You saw the sign for Shangri La, yes?"

The tourist nods his head excitedly.

"That's the old National Museum. Now it's a theme hotel, with an amusement park and cultural shows going on all day long, all draped in Muzak's audio architecture. You can even get up on stage in the Gurung Ghar and do a karaoke version of 'Simsime pani' to the accompaniment of virtual Gurung musicians," she says dismissively. "I don't recommend it."

"Christineji," I say. "You never saw old museum? It was no place special. I like to ride the Machhapuchhre. Better than to look at those dolls wearing tiny ethnic costumes."

The tourist looks puzzled.

Christine shrugs. "The National Museum is the heart of the Swayambhu City. Once the Oberoi started doing business there, a whole town grew up along the road from Chhauni to Swayambhu—that's the big Buddhist stupa on the hill, yes? People selling food, crack, trinkets, whatever. It's changing fast, even though the government tries to control growth. Some of it's not bad. But it's mostly gaudy representations and cheap imitations. And all the different theme bars run by same corporation. Same one that own the Hard Rock Cafe in Nagarkot. And what do the stupid 'about town' writers at the *Kathmandu Post* say? 'Exotic! First-class! Wild adventure!' Fuck it. I say your best bet is to go out to Bauddha, the stupa on the other side of town. There's a restaurant there, been making the best *kursani* pizza in town since the '50s."

Werner shakes his head and comments, "Bitte, I like Swayambhu City. Ja, the shows are silly, aber natürlich some good restaurants there. If you want treat, you maybe try the Yeti Delight at the Sherpa Hut."

Perhaps more confused than before, the man thanks us and heads back outside. "Beware the wrath of the goddess!" yells Werner jokingly to him from the window, helpfully pointing the way down the street toward the west and the glittery pleasure domes of Swayambhu City. Christine's finger hovers over the "record" button on her Sony as Werner settles back onto his stool.

* * *

We arrived at Wal-Mart the next day just in time to see the Wal-Mart employees doing a cheer.

"Wa diu! A diu! La diu! Squiggly diu! Ma diu! A diu! Ra diu! Tha diu! Ke banchha? Wal-Mart! Numbar ek ko ho? Gaahakji! Numbar ek ko ho? Kyastomar!"

I read about this ritual at the Wal-Mart Visitor Center that I told you about in Arkansas. One of the displays in the old Walton's 5 & 10—the original version of Wal-Mart, converted into a "walk through the company's looking glass"—explained that

Sam Walton had visited a tennis ball factory in Korea and noticed that the workers took a break every morning to do a company cheer along with some exercises. Sam loved that and devised a cheer for his "associates." And to think that it took the insidious corporate strategies of the East to teach the West how to produce a superficially happy labor force. Sam called it his "whistle while you work" philosophy. I don't know. I prefer a good game of chess every now and then.

Anyway, I was telling you about the Wal-Mart opening. It was a little more than half an hour before five o'clock. There was already a large crowd there, and it took no small effort to part the sea of people to drive our truck up to the side of the stage. We unloaded our equipment—being particularly careful with my amp, which already had our little bomb rigged up inside—onto the temporary stage, which was decorated with red, white, and blue paper pinned up with crossed American and Nepali flags. As we set up our gear, smooth sax lines started oozing out of one of the speakers. It sounded like Marsalis, but when I looked up at the giant television screen which had been installed for the event, I saw video footage of the former U.S. President, Bill Clinton, playing the saxophone. At the time, I recalled that I had seen a display in Bentonville that described the grand opening of the Wal-Mart Visitor Center, at which Clinton, then the governor of Arkansas, played the saxophone. I wondered how much money Clinton was getting for his virtual appearance here. Probably much more than my band was getting.

With about fifteen minutes to go before five o'clock, we were ready for a sound check. The crowd was starting to seem a bit impatient, and we were too hasty. Our first song, "Hotel California," was replete with the squawks and yelps of feedback. The crowd didn't seem to mind, though, so we lit into a version of "All Along the Watchtower" that sounded like it fit somewhere between Dylan's version of the song, Hendrix's version, and Dylan's version of Hendrix's version. By the time we settled on a final chord, a blue-vested Wal-Mart representative on stage was getting pretty antsy, as he had given us a signal to stop about halfway through the piece. We ignored him. Although I often close my eyes when I sing, for the rest of this song I was avidly watching the antics of the Wal-Mart Kathmandu mascot out in the crowd, who was wearing an ape suit—or perhaps it was meant to be an abominable snowman costume—and a giant yellow smiley head with a cowboy hat. The blue-vested man on stage kept trying to get us to stop, and the mascot, bouncing through the crowd and shaking hands with bemused Nepalis, kept extravagantly miming the shushing actions of the Wal-Mart representative. By the time we finished, the whole crowd had picked up his joking imitations and was gesturing for us to stop at the same time that they were screaming for us to continue.

The video screen hummed back into action then, and the crowd began to quiet down. A ten-foot-tall video image of His Majesty King Birendra Bir Bikram Shah Dev appeared, offering, in Nepali, his congratulations and best wishes for an auspicious grand opening. We set down our instruments and stepped to the side of the stage; I leaned against the stage railing, putting my hands in my jeans pockets. My right hand found the detonator while my face struggled to make my pose look natural. The king's speech was followed by a short cartoon featuring Ganesh and Jesus flying, hand in hand, toward a Wal-Mart store. Ganesh was flapping his ears Dumbo-style, while Jesus was simply levitating through the air. As they hovered over the store, Ganesh sprinkled some sparkling and presumably holy substance over it, and Jesus shot a ray of light out from his palm onto the roof of the store, which began glowing either ethereally or radioactively—the animation wasn't particularly adept. As Ganesh and Jesus floated off into the sunset, a neon Wal-Mart logo flashed on and off above a phrase carved in animated vine-entwined stone, reading "aggressive hospitality."

The sunset scene faded out, and a short video clip of Sam Walton came on; I knew these were to be the final spoken words of the inauguration ceremony for the new Wal-Mart store. I remember them well. The speech itself was the one that Sam made when he accepted the Medal of Freedom from U.S. President George Bush shortly before he died. "And we'll lower the cost of living for everyone," he pronounced boldly, "not just in America, but we'll give the world an op. . . ." The screen fizzled. I looked over at our equipment. The lights on the amps went dark.

Electricity was pretty scarce in those days; often there wasn't enough to go around, and there were scheduled load-sharing times. This outage wasn't scheduled, but I can't say it was unusual. The members of The Instigators—that was the name of my band—looked questioningly at each other. We realized that our little explosion wouldn't make much sense without any electricity flowing through the line.

Then I saw the Wal-Mart mascot, still smiling for all he was worth, race to the back of the stage. The clock tower sent out the first few notes of its prelude to five o'clock. I'm sure I tensed visibly. But then, I heard the cranking of a gasoline engine from the back of the stage, and as it throttled upwards, I realized that it was a generator. So the Wal-Mart folks weren't entirely unprepared. The television screen snapped back to life, and Sam continued, ". . . portunity to see what it's like to save and have a better lifestyle, a better life for all."

Five o'clock clanged around just as he came to the word, "lifestyle." A modest explosion popped out of my amplifier and died. The smiley face of the mascot, who was bending over the generator, betrayed no surprise at all, but he jumped like a spooked rat. At "better life for all," a much more powerful blast on the other side of town rocked the street beneath us and echoed back and forth between the walls of the old royal palace and the hotels that decorated the northern fringe of Freak Street. A few people began to panic. My band took up their instruments, and we plunged into a too-fast rendition of Jimmy Cliff's "You Can Get It If You Really Want." The crowd shimmered in place for a moment, ready either to burst into fragments or collapse in upon itself.

From down Freak Street, we heard a thunderous clamor of yelling voices, stamping feet, and revving engines. Then another bomb ripped out the back of the Wal-Mart. A mob of people came pouring out of Freak Street—on foot, on bicycles, on motorcycles, in Tempos. While the stage parted much of the human sea, it wasn't long before waves of people started crashing up and across the stage. We couldn't help but be pulled into their wake as they smashed through the front doors of the store, grabbed what they could on their way down the aisles, and spilled out the hole in the back of the store. Holding tightly to my guitar with one hand, yet trying to avoid being strangled by its strap, I was sucked into the store, pushed and pulled past a headless Ronald McDonald, through an aisle of pots and pans, and out the back of the store. I secured only a handful of Hello Kitty bookbags with my free hand, but at least when I was deposited back on the street I still had my guitar.

There was no crowd lingering at the back of the store. This was clearly a well-organized disturbance; people were simply flooding through Durbar Square and draining down the streets that connected to it. I forded streams of merchandise-laden pedestrians and vehicles to reach the Shiva-Parvati temple, where I clambered up the steps and sat down to watch. Despite the ebb and flow of people below, all seemed strangely silent. I lit a cigarette and watched the tendrils of smoke ascend toward a nirvana with the smoke from the explosions and the exhaust of the vehicles. I sat for quite some time, thinking about the holes these bombs had made, opening up paths that none of us previously could have envisioned. My amp was gone. The Wal-Mart was a quickly emptying concrete shell. I got up and went back down to street level, taking care to do *puja* to Ganesh before heading back to Thamel.

I found my band sprawled around a new green plastic table on the roof of the Hotel Mount Fuji. We went back to the ruins of the Wal-Mart store later that evening and managed to salvage a few pieces of equipment. Our truck was a bit dented in spots, but we drove it out of there. I think I ran over the mascot's discarded smiley face. It was dark and one of the headlights had been smashed, so I couldn't tell for sure. On our way out of there, the working headlight momentarily picked out the grinning head of Ronald McDonald, lying in the gutter. Indra thought his apparent glee over having been decapitated was hilarious and tried out imitations of his grin on us all the way back to Thamel.

Nepalis and foreigners were still milling about, ecstatic with the guilty thrill of destruction and unsure what to do with their unspent energy. We decided some Talking Heads wouldn't hurt. Friends brought equipment for us to replace what we had lost in the riots, and we spent the night burning down the house. Most of the police were busy dealing with the aftermath of the explosions, and they didn't stop us.

* * *

Christine interrupts. "*Mahesh dai,* you said that there was one explosion on the other side of town. What was that?"

Lili, this leathery old Hawai'ian hippie who lives in the flat above my store, had wandered in earlier, and was squatting by the door. She answered for me. "That was the old Keshar Library. The city was going to destroy it anyway, to make way for a new IMAX theater. I was working then for a movie crew, an NGO called the Filmi Visions Group. We had been asked by the city to document the building, the grounds, and the workers' lives before the building was to be destroyed. We were mostly just a front for the Tibetan Mafia, but we did a few beautiful ethnographic films. You know, like old Edmund Carpenter said, 'We use media to destroy cultures, but we first use media to create a false record of what we are about to destroy.' Only in this case the Maoists managed to destroy the Keshar Library before we could finish. The explosion was meant to draw the attention of the army and the police while the real action was going down in Freak Street."

"Eh," says Christine. "I understand now. I knew the second royal palace was turned into the big cineplex, but I never knew where Keshar Library was before. It was over to the west of the palace itself, where the Bollywood Bomb sitting now?"

"Hajur," I say. "They decide to make the bomb into a theme of the cinema hall. At first, was supposed to be for Hollywood films. But Hollywood soon go into computer-based entertainment. Interactive simulations, like Disney does at the Enchanted Tiki Room in Swayambhu City. B4U take over the hall, show Bombay, London, and Toronto films."

Werner adds, "Ja, und schauen good movies. I see one gestern. Like ze French film you see, confuse the question of identity."

"Better that than watching those fixed identities getting pumped out of Swayambhu City," mutters Christine. "*Mahesh dai,* how your story finish?"

* * *

The next morning, I walked down to the Wal-Mart. The army was already clearing the rubble away. As you know, they tore it down completely, and very little has been heard of Wal-Mart in Nepal since. I peeked into the remains of the store; there was almost nothing left. Almost every single item had been stripped from the shelves and injected into the bloodstream of Kathmandu the previous evening. It was sad, in a way, to see this great temple to American-style capitalism desecrated and looted. Invigorating, too, to realize that Kathmandu's future would not necessarily be envisioned first outside of Nepal, then dumped ceremoniously upon us. I stood in the middle of the plaza, one of many people savoring the possibilities that swirled in the fog amid those ruins of a summer morning.

Like I said, I had been thinking even then of giving up my music. It seemed as if it had served its purpose. I remember walking up toward Indrachok, thinking about what I might do instead. Not really paying attention to where I was going, I ran into Ricky Martin right outside my shop here. He was really nice—he said he really liked our sound. I told him about the Menudo song we were going to do for him, and he sounded surprised, said that he didn't expect anyone to remember his life before "Livin' la Vida Loca." Then he laughed and confessed that sometimes he himself didn't remember his earlier life, either. As he said goodbye and continued on down the street, I stood for a moment, looking up at nothing in particular. My eyes came to rest on the window of this shop. A few years later, I began renting it out. I've been right here since, and, with Laxmi's good wishes, I'll continue selling my carpets and boxes here. I don't know if I like what Kathmandu is becoming. But it is my home. As long as our shrink-wrapped and price-tagged parodies of culture continue to lure foreign money here, I'm content to sit here on the edge of this sea of tourists and fish out the occasional customer.

* * *

Werner left the head of Ronald McDonald with me. I guess he decided it might hold more memories for me than it did for him. I had to insist that he take a small but very nice blue carpet in exchange. That was just over five years ago. Christine went back to Indonesia later that year amid tears and flowers, promising that she'd be back very soon. The chess set I keep at the store has remained in its box ever since.

After a good cleaning and some touch-up painting, Ronald's head took up residence on a shelf in my house, surrounded by the smaller curios and mementos my wife has accumulated. Ronald avoids looking out the window at the recklessly built hotel that teetered up across the street last year. But sometimes, late at night, as the distant sounds of Swayambhu City sneak in through the window, I like to watch Ronald's shiny red plastic hair reflect the hotel's dancing lights. As I look at his head now, though, my eyes linger on the faded garland of purple flowers that hangs down from what little neck he has, remnants of last year's *bhai tika*. It will be *bhai tika* again soon, a time when sisters and ritually adopted sisters return to their homes to wish their brothers long life. Perhaps this is the year that Christine will return to Nepal.

I finish my whiskey, pull down the shade, and join my wife in bed. I don't know. I wonder what traces of Nepal are preserved in Christine. Maybe she's forgotten us. She could at least write occasionally.

The Last Time Tere Danced a Rumba

RUTH BEHAR

Author's Note: The following text is an extract from Night-gowns from Cuba, *a novel-in-progress. The novel is a mix of autobiography, ethnography, and fiction. It examines the lives of three generations of women in a Jewish-Cuban family as seen from the perspective of an Afro-Cuban woman who was employed by the family as a domestic worker in the years before the Cuban revolution of 1959. The extract focuses on the pivotal year of 1954, when the narrator's sister had to make a major decision about whether to continue in her job as a domestic worker or marry. The religion of Santería is the cosmological setting of the story, and the deity of Olokún, who inhabits the depths of the ocean and cannot be represented in visual form, haunts the narrative, which ties together Jewish-Cuban and Afro-Cuban histories and desires.*

It was the summer of 1954. . . . The letters from Europe with news of death had long since been tied with bits and pieces of satin ribbon and put away in perfumed drawers where they could detonate softly. There was nothing more for the Levi family to fear. Those they had lost in the war were lost forever, and they, who had gotten on boats to Cuba and created families on

179

this island, had grown strong and prospered. They had prospered enough to have black women like myself and my sister Tere work in their households.

Tragedy overtook them and it came in a form unforeseen and unforeseeable, and unalterable. If Eleggúa closes a door, no amount of cigar smoke, candies, and *aguardiente* can open it again. And so it was that in the summer of 1954 the Levi family learned that the death of Ariel was imminent and that all the medicine, money, and love in the world could not save him. For months Ariel had complained of pains when walking or standing too long. Natán and Rita had taken him to the best doctors in La Habana, who knew about every possible illness of the legs and feet, but they'd not found anything wrong with him. Then he'd started to grow unusually tired and he started saying he didn't want to go to school anymore. Rita grew impatient with her son and told Tere one night that she wondered if he was pretending to be ill to get attention, but Tere, who knew the boy well, said that Ariel was not that kind of child and that he was lately so drowsy he was falling asleep while eating his meals. Finally Natán and Rita got on a plane with Arielito and went to an important hospital in Minnesota, where they say the cold never lets up, not even in the summer, and there discovered the ugly truth: the child was suffering from leukemia, an illness for which there was no cure. Rita told Naomi that on the plane ride home she prayed for a crash, so as not to have to return to Cuba to face the extinction of her son from this earth. He was only eleven, the boy, and the big doctors in Minnesota said he would be gone before his twelfth birthday.

It was also in the summer of 1954, and this is why I remember the date clearly, that my sister Tere received a proposal of marriage. Amado had been courting her for years. He was a pretty-faced mulatto and worked as a chauffeur for the ambassador of Peru, who lived down the street from Natán and Rita in Miramar. He wanted Tere to marry him and leave her job as a maid so she could attend to him and the needs of the children they would surely have in good time. He said the ambassador of Peru held him in high regard and promised to pay for the wedding party, including a gown for Tere, and give him a generous wedding gift. He told Tere he adored her, but he didn't want to wait for her to make up her mind. If she loved him as he loved her, there was nothing to think about, no reason for doubts or delays.

Tere was twenty-eight and voluptuous, with good hips for dancing the rumba and cradling babies. She had always said that if she reached the age of thirty without getting married, then she'd never marry afterward. My sister Tere is like that: she utters pronouncements and then lives by them. But how she suffered during the summer of 1954! Of course I can't forget that date. Arielito was dying and the destiny of my sister Tere was being determined by the ancestors, the *orishas,* and the muleheadedness of her own will. She wanted to marry Amado, because she did love him, but she had known Arielito since birth, and the thought of abandoning him to an indifferent caretaker, just when he needed her most, caused her tremendous pain.

We chose a Sunday not long after Tere had received the marriage proposal and Ariel's illness had been diagnosed to seek advice from our father and his *padrino* in Agramonte. We went prepared with candies for Elegguá, white flowers for Obbatalá, sugary rum cakes for Ochún, and red candles for Changó. The bus ride from La Habana to Agramonte no longer made my stomach sick. I'd become used to traveling on buses around the city, so they had ceased to be a novelty to my body. Tired from the week's work, Tere and I fell asleep as soon as the bus left the station.

There was sweat on my brow from the summer sun beating through the window, but I awoke refreshed, as did Tere. We gathered up our packages and daintily took hold of the black patent leather handbags with the shiny silver clasps that Natán Levi had given each of us the previous Christmas. Remembering our city manners, we thanked the bus driver for the pleasant ride and he returned the favor by ogling at our rumps as we stepped off the bus. In Agramonte the first person we encountered was Anselmo returning from his fields with an enormous cluster of green bananas. We bought the entire cluster from him, to give as an offering to Changó, who is the owner of the banana, the fruit that sustains the poorest of the poor and keeps them from starving to death.

Our father was at the kitchen table sorting through a mound of rice. I felt strange seeing him engaged in this woman's work. But with my mother long gone and only my brothers left in Agramonte, there wasn't a woman in my father's house to do the woman's work. Self-reproach stabbed at my soul. I, as the youngest daughter, my mother's ninth and the one who sucked at her breasts the longest, had not kept my obligation to stay with my father and care for him. Ten years had passed since I'd left for La Habana and I knew that I would not return to Agramonte again to live. All the country people I met in La Habana—and what maid, gardener, cook, or chauffeur in that sea-ravished city wasn't from the country?—said they would never return home to their towns and villages, that they'd been seduced by the charms of La Habana and they'd stay forever, even if they had to beg at the door of the cathedral. Tere and I only returned to Agramonte now three times a year, for New Year's Day in January, for the anniversary of our mother's death in April, and for our father's *fiesta de santo* for Changó on the 4th of December. When we could, we also liked to return to Agramonte a second time in December, to be there on the 16th and 17th of the month for the town's celebration of San Lázaro, the powerful Babalu-Ayé of our African ancestors, who protects those who are ill and lame. That second visit in December depended on the phases of the moon and the Jewish calendar and when the Janucá holiday fell and whether my sister Tere and I were needed by the Levi family to peel and shred potatoes for the special pancakes they ate with sugar on that holiday. But this visit, in the middle of July, was totally unexpected.

"Papi, here, let me clean the rice," I said, dropping my packages on the table and pulling up a seat next to my father.

"Yeyita, *tranquila*, I'm doing fine," he replied in his good-natured way. "You and Tere go greet the *santos* and then we can talk."

I followed Tere into the room of the *santos,* carrying the cluster of green bananas for Changó, which I placed at the foot of my father's *batá* drums. The air in that room was like no other. It smelled of flowers and fruits left for the *santos,* and candle wax, and tobacco, and honey, and the memory of blood, and the breath of the dead and the living. I always felt an immediate sense of peace and protection upon entering that room. Tere opened the cabinet below the Christian *santos* and exposed the enamel basins filled with the sacred stones of the *fundamentos,* which our ancestors had brought with them from Africa in the slave ships. Tere kneeled first and she picked up one bell at a time to call each of the *santos,* and when she was done I did the same. I can imagine what Tere must have asked of the *santos,* but I made sure to ask on her behalf as well, to pray for an easy and clear resolution to the indecision that was tormenting her, about whether to marry the man she loved and would surely lose if she refused, or continue caring for the sick boy who loved her and would soon be lost to the world.

Afterward we went about preparing the rice and the black beans and roasting a chicken and frying the plantains, and we made an enormous dish of okra breaded with eggs and flour to give as an offering to Changó, of which we kept a small part for ourselves. My father and I ate with pleasure and vigor, but Tere, who was not one to eat much anyway, barely touched the food on her plate.

"Tere, what's troubling you?" our father asked.

She shook her head and brought her hand to her mouth as if wanting to keep the words from springing out on their own. She would not speak and so I spoke for her.

"Papi, there is a good man who wants to marry Tere. He's a chauffeur for the ambassador of Peru, a hard-working man. He says that Tere will not need to work as a maid if she marries him. He won't let her work as a maid if she marries him! He says he loves her and that if she loves him, she should not make him wait even a minute for the response he hopes for."

"And do you love him, Tere?"

Tears rolled down her cheeks. "Yes, Papi," she said.

"So what is the problem? You know that I have faith in your judgment. Besides, you are a grown woman. If you want this man for a husband, I will not stand in your way."

"But I can't marry him," Tere said, her lower lip trembling. "I can't marry him. I can't marry him right now."

Tere wept as I'd never seen her weep.

Again I spoke for Tere. "The reason Tere feels she can't get married now is that Arielito is very sick. Natán and Rita took him to doctors in Minnesota and the boy has leukemia and will not live long. It may be a few weeks or a few months, but he won't make it to his twelfth birthday."

Tere continued to weep. My father had lit a cigar and was listening attentively. In the quietest of whispers, as if babies were asleep in the room and might waken, he said, "Go on, Yeya."

"Not that the boy knows he's dying. Or, if he knows, he pretends not to. I think that's the worst thing they're doing, but who am I to question their wisdom? Natán and Rita have chosen not to tell Ariel or his sister Anita that the situation of the boy is hopeless. They keep saying he will be better, much better, by the time he reaches his thirteenth birthday, which among the Hebrews is the age when boys are given a big party and start to be treated as men. Like the *quinceañeras* we give to girls when they turn fifteen and become young women. Except that for Arielito, there will be no party, and he will never become a man."

Tere wiped the tears from her face with the tips of her fingers. She finally spoke.

"The poor child needs me. His mother doesn't understand him the way I do. If he eats anything at all, it's thanks to my efforts and patience. He sleeps best when I'm at his bedside, stroking his hair. I tell you, I've spent so many hours helping him on his homework that I think I've taught him more Yiddish and Hebrew than his teachers at the Centro Israelita. And it's for me that he most likes to play his accordion. His eyes light up from seeing me clap after he's played a few melodies."

"Tere," our father interrupted, and for a moment he didn't know how to go on. He puffed on his cigar and then said, "Your feelings for Arielito are worthy of admiration, but for the sake of Arielito, a child who is not yours and could never be yours, would you give up the promise of your own happiness? Would you give up the children that would come from your own womb by marrying a man who loves you?"

"I don't know," she said. "I don't know."

"Tere, you must never forget that you're a paid worker at the house of Natán Levi. We know the Levi family because they lived here in Agramonte, and *el viejo* Abram won our respect and Máximo Glinienski our trust. The Levi family has been good to you and Yeya. I don't deny that. It's natural for you to feel attached to that family. It's natural for you to want to stay with them during this time when the God of their ancestors has withdrawn their blessings. But that family is not your family. Today or tomorrow, if they find another black woman who will do the same work you do at half the pay, they won't hesitate to let you go. No one who works for money is indispensable. Remember that. Then where will you be, Teresita? I know you don't want to come back to Agramonte to help me cut sugarcane." With those words, said with earnestness rather than bitterness, our father took a last puff of his cigar and put out the stub in the ashtray I had quickly brought to him from the front room the moment I saw he was about to drop it on the floor.

"I don't know why Amado can't wait a little. He's being so impatient," said Tere, sighing.

If Tere was hoping for sympathy from our father, she didn't get the smallest drop of it. "And why should a man wait for a woman any longer than he has to? Your mother didn't wait a minute to tell me she would be my wife. I think Amado has all the reason in the world to ask you to make up your mind now. Waiting won't do any good. If there is fire in the love you have for each other, then you shouldn't let it grow cold."

Tere didn't answer. She had no more tears to shed and her gaze, always so thoughtful and expressive, was suddenly hollow. Our father, who could never bear to see any of his children sad, saw how deep was her disappointment and said she should not base such an important decision on what he, merely an ordinary human being, thought. He told her she should consult with the *orishas* and hear what they had to tell her through the *ekele* divination of his *padrino.*

Our father excused himself and said he needed to sleep a siesta after such a hearty and satisfying lunch. Tere and I took off our stockings and high-heeled city shoes and changed into old sandals—not those Máximo Glinienski made for us, which had long since worn out, but others purchased with our own money in La Habana that we kept on either side of the bed we had shared in our girlhood. And so we set off for Victor's house on the dirt road at the far end of the town, past the railroad station. It was such a hot July day that even the flies were too tired to buzz. They stuck to your skin and rolled off when you swatted them. Tere and I walked slowly through the town, greeting people who'd known us all our lives. Not a single door was closed because everyone was trying to take advantage of the fresher air that might waft in from outside and release the steam from the houses. From each home the sound of the rocking chairs swaying to and fro was like a heartbeat pulsing through the town, marking the steady and brutal passage of time.

My father's *padrino,* Victor Elizondo, or Chacho, as everyone had called him since the days of his youth, was the oldest *babalawo* in Agramonte. He had very dark black satiny skin that gleamed with the memory of Africa. People said he was a child when slavery was abolished in Cuba. He could remember the day they heard the news in Agramonte and how the elders, in gratitude, sacrificed doves, chickens, and goats, and the drums did not stop sounding for an entire week, and there was an abundance of food, and not a soul went hungry, and all of the *orishas* descended, and people ate and sang and danced until they collapsed from the exhaustion of being free. He said that a *toque* like that would never be seen again. And should never be seen again, even if it was a *toque* of extravagant beauty and passion, because slavery was the vilest thing that had ever been created by human beings. Expressing gratitude for its end only once, until the end of time, was enough.

Chacho was nearly blind from cataracts. On the day he was received as a *babalawo,* it was revealed that he would eventually go blind and that he was not to try to prevent it, either by herbal remedies or the surgery of doctors, because if he did a yet worse fate would befall him. As is true of blind people, he had a strong sense of smell and the delicate hearing of a musician. We'd barely approached his house or said a word and he was already greeting us by our names. He was sitting very still in a rocking chair in the small porch at the entrance to his house, his hands folded on his lap.

"Teresita and Yeyita, what brings you to me on this hot afternoon when there isn't a soul out in the street?"

We each hugged and kissed him. I was about to speak for Tere and say we'd come for a *consulta,* but that turned out not to be necessary. As we stood on either side of him, he passed the palm of his hand gently over Tere's brow and cheeks and said he could tell she'd been weeping and that something was troubling her. He shook his head and rose from his rocking chair and asked us to please follow him inside. In a room next to the kitchen he kept his *santos* and a large altar draped in purple for San Lázaro, or Babalú Ayé, who was his guardian saint and the saint he'd received and been crowned with when he took the path of the *orishas.* There, he offered consultations to all those who felt they needed to ask the *orishas* for guidance in how to move forward in their lives. In those days, *consultas* were taken seriously and sought only for the most vitally important matters of health, prosperity, and the clamoring of the heart. No self-respecting *babalawo* would ever have charged a fee, as they do nowadays, to the great shame of the *orishas.* Chacho was our father's *padrino,* of course, but even if he had not been so, he was incapable of requesting money for anything that concerned the *orishas.*

He sat down at his consulting table and told us to bring over the two chairs that were by the wall. From his pocket he pulled out the pouch in which he kept the *ekele.* He laid it on the table and felt the flat beads, connected to each other by a thin silver chain, to be sure they were positioned correctly. Then he gave

Tere a seashell and a small smooth rock and told her to juggle them and put each one in a different hand and not to show him what was in either hand until he told her to. Over and over he picked up the *ekele* and let it fall on the table, and with every throw he'd ask Tere to juggle the shell and the stone and see in which hand each ended up. Finally, he stopped and said he saw the pattern. He would tell her what it was, unless she first had any questions to ask of the oracle. Tere turned and looked at me and I told her that I could not speak for her, not now, that she should ask if she wanted to know.

"Chacho, there is a man who wants to marry me," she began, but she didn't have to finish her sentence.

"Yes," said Chacho. "And you should marry him. The *orishas* say you are at a crossroads and that you must choose the path of love. Ochún herself speaks here in the *ekele* and says that you will have her protection if you give yourself to the path of love, that you have nothing to fear because everything will go well for you. The *orishas* say you will have a happy marriage, if you marry now, and children who will care for you in your old age. The sign that you got is an unusual one and asks that you not neglect the demands of your heart, because if you do, you will suffer greatly later in life from pains in your heart so severe they will take your breath away. Your sign also says that you are to stay away from hospitals and cemeteries, to be careful not to have too much contact with those who are sick and dying, and to keep your distance from the dead. If ever you must go to a funeral, do not stay long, because the soul of a dead person will stick to you like glue. So, Teresita, now you know what the *orishas* have to say. Listen to them, and especially to Ochún, and you will keep sadness and suffering from entering your life. I suggest you light a candle for Ochún tonight at your father's house and pray to her with devotion. Wear something yellow, even just a kerchief, to show her that you need her blessing on the path of love."

"But Chacho, the boy I am taking care of in La Habana is dying. How can I leave him?" Tere was crying again.

"The boy certainly must have great affection for you, Teresita, because you have known him since birth and have attended to him with intelligence and devotion. But he has his mother and father, doesn't he? Teresita, don't disobey Ochún. She's very impulsive, very moody, and she's capable of withdrawing all of her protection in a second if you refuse it when she offers it to you."

We left Chacho's house with heavy feet. Night had fallen and the heat was a little less thick. Tere was sullen and I thought I would try to cheer her. I told Tere that she should be feeling pleased that the *orishas* were on the side of her getting married. Wasn't that what she really wanted to do? Didn't she love Amado? He was such a good man and loved her and treated her like a lady. With him, she would have her own house and not have to be a maid in the house of strangers. Yes, it would be difficult to leave the house of Natán and Rita at this moment with Arielito so sick, but surely they would understand that she had to move forward in her life, that if she waited very much longer she would be too old to bear children of her own. And as I said that, I realized there was no way for Tere to say she wanted children of her own without it sounding cold and cruel to Natán and Rita, who were about to lose their only son.

We had turned on to our street and could hear the call of the drums. The drums were sounding for Changó, and the hands coaxing the music from the animal skins and the carved wood were unmistakably those of my father. Tere trembled as we approached the house. She did not like *bembés,* as I did, and had always kept her distance when the drumming and dancing and trancing got too animated. But no sooner had we entered the courtyard, where several neighbors had already assembled, than Tere began to dance, at first slowly and deliberately, and then faster, abandoning herself to the rhythm of the drums, which were now being played not only by our father but by two other men who'd joined him to complete the trio of the *batá* drummers. Tere was a good dancer and in La Habana she often went with Amado to the dance halls that existed for mulattos in those days. But the kind of rumba she was letting go that night didn't resemble in the least the controlled and numbered steps she took in the dance halls. She shook her shoulders and exaggerated the movement of her hips. Her hair, which that same morning before leaving La Habana she had straightened and neatly shaped into soft curls that lightly touched the nape of her neck, was now loose and wild and frizzy from the burning heat that was emanating from her own body. I had never seen her dance that way before and would never see her dance that way again. It was a dance of such longing and such desperation that it made you want to cry to watch her. At the same time, she looked beautiful, radiant, sensual, womanly. The drums were sounding for Changó that night, but my sister Tere had been possessed by Ochún, the least governable and most stunning of Changó's wives, and the only woman *orisha* of our whole pantheon that could put no limits on her need to love and love and love. One of our neighbors, I don't remember if it was Mercedita, managed to tie a yellow kerchief around Tere's neck as she danced. She danced for a long time, and when she was done the rumba ended and everyone went home.

Tere didn't light a candle that night for Ochún. My father and I helped her to bed and the next morning she took the yellow kerchief off, folded it carefully, and put it in the handbag that Natán Levi had given her for Christmas the year before. It wasn't until we stepped off the bus in La Habana that she told me she'd made up her mind. She would not marry Amado. She would stay with Arielito for as long as it took him to die.

It was another three months before Ariel died. And in that time Amado went from being distressed that he'd lost Tere to finding another woman who did not hesitate for a second when he asked her to marry him. *Si te vas, te juro que busco a otra,* as that *son montuno* goes. "If you leave, I promise I'll find someone else." Tere stuck by her decision. She never wavered again. By the time Ariel was buried in the Jewish cemetery that the *polacos* had built in Guanabacoa, she knew she would never marry, never live with a man, never bear children. Ariel went to his grave and Tere held on to her virginity like a precious jewel. For women of our color and our class, that was an unusual jewel to own. As a perpetual virgin, Tere acquired the power to see through lies, to know the secrets that others worked so diligently to hide. But this only became apparent to me in the future, long after the coming of the revolution and many years after the Levi family had left Cuba.

How quickly I can tell the story now, so many years later, faster than I can sneeze. In reality, those months passed slowly and they were painful in their slowness. All of us knew that Ariel was dying, except for Ariel himself and his sister Anita. What hard work it was to keep the truth from them. The pity lodged itself in my throat like a stone.

Those doctors in Minnesota predicted the exact course that Ariel's illness would take and they were so correct in everything they said would happen to the child that, for the first time in my life, I realized that there is cruelty in knowledge. The doctors said that Ariel would go from being tired and feeling heavy-footed, in the early stage of his illness, to suddenly feeling energetic again, as if he were recovering his health. But they warned that we were not to take his seeming recovery as a sign that all was well. No, he would shortly move into the next stage, in which he would grow fat and bloated, uncomfortably inflated, like a balloon at the point of bursting. He would grow tired once more. And then, the final, and worst, stage would follow: he would be in pain, day and night, insufferable pain, and he would have to suffer it, suffer the insufferable pain, which would strike his entire body, the doctors said.

This pain, for which there were neither words nor medicines, would lead him to shout out in exasperation that even the hair on his head hurt. It made no difference that Tere was gentle with the comb, the boy would cry and yell and giggle, all at the same time, exclaiming, "Have you ever heard of such a thing? How can the hair on one's head hurt? My hair hurts. Not my head, but my hair! It feels as if all the ships from the port of La Habana are using my hair to tie their anchors down. Ay, Tere, how it hurts. Every single strand hurts."

Tere gave herself wholeheartedly to Ariel's every need and desire. She became obsessed with caring for his hair and gradually she was able to make the pain he had felt go away. Each day she rinsed his hair with a different kind of water: rain water, ocean water, clear water in which white *azucenas* had soaked for hours, water fragrant with the peel of sweet oranges, water smoothened with the essence of coconut, water enriched with beaten egg yolks, and holy water, of which neither Rita nor Natán Levi knew, that came from the shrine of San Lázaro, our Babalu-Ayé, in the town of Rincón. The doctors predicted Ariel's hair would turn thin and mangy and fall out. But with Tere's treatments his hair grew more golden and beautiful as his illness worsened. Everyone who encountered him in the street had to utter a compliment about his hair. In the sun it shone like honey just gathered from the hive.

As Ariel's appetite withered, Tere strove to provide him with all the nourishing foods he loved. She whipped powdered chocolate into creamy milk that she ordered from Miguelito, who delivered it fresh from the countryside of Havana. She prepared very fine, exquisite *papas fritas* that she'd form into a bird's nest and present to him on a big round serving dish. She cut his steak into pieces so tiny and dainty that moths could have eaten it. In the mornings, she'd go to the *gallegos* and get him *churros,* the long curly strips of dough all crisp and sugary, and in the afternoons, while he napped, she'd run out to the *barrio chino* and bring him pintfuls of the exotic ice cream flavors of the Orient, made from spices like ginger or fruits like lichee, to surprise him with new flavors he'd not known existed.

Of course Natán and Rita lavished upon their son all the attentions and pleasures of both their great love and their bountiful wealth. How those two parents adored their son, how they melted with affection for him. They exhaled when he did, they gritted their teeth when he did. Lightly, as if they were newborn doves, they held his pudgy hands in their own. They bought him so many incredible gifts in those sunset days—a shiny red bicycle that came from England and had three speeds, an electric train set that had dozens of cars and a track that could circle around their entire marble-tiled living room, and, most spectacular of all, a new professional accordion, from which Ariel coaxed sounds that released the hidden beauty of the nectar of flowers.

The boy had played the piano since he was five, and his teacher said he had a very good ear for music, but before he became ill, he simply sounded like a well-disciplined child obediently playing the notes written on the page. After his illness, with the new accordion to accompany him, he began to sing heartbreaking tango songs about lost love. Innocence allowed him to sing tenderly of experiences he would never have. So talented was he that he was invited to play on the radio several times. But Tere says he sang and played best and most forcefully at home, before going to bed. Dressed in his pajamas, his glasses off, and his eyes focused inward, he would grasp the accordion in his plump arms and the music sounded so unearthly that it would frighten Tere, who was certain that Ariel was performing for the guardian angel that was visible to no one but him.

Tere, watching Ariel with his parents in the evenings when they returned from work at their store, would fight the tears that wanted to form in her eyes. Later, alone in her bed, she would let loose and weep her stifled tears, but silently, because in those last months and weeks she slept in the same room with Ariel, who often awoke in the night, needing to go to the bathroom or to give voice to the dreams that accumulated in his young boy's head as his life was ending.

What fantastic dreams the boy shared with Tere in the thick of night. The dream that haunted him, toward the end, came in September and October, in the days of the Jewish new year. He'd heard from his teachers at the Centro Israelita that their Jewish god had an enormous book in which, as the new year arrived, he would write down the names of all the Jewish people scattered about the world who would continue to be alive in the year to come. In his dream, Ariel would see their Jewish god shutting the book before his own name had been written down. He'd be begging and begging him to please open the book again and add his name and he would awaken spelling out the five letters of his name and telling his Jewish god that it wouldn't take very much time to open the book and record his name with the others. Tere spent many nights holding the frantic boy in her arms until he fell asleep from exhaustion. He always urged her never to say anything about the dream to his parents. He knew they didn't want him to know he was dying, but dreams never lie and his dreams revealed the terrible truth to him. Yet for the sake of not hurting his parents, he pretended until the very end that he was unaware of the fate that was his. He trusted Tere to keep his secret. She told only me, her younger sister, about what the boy knew. I, who would cut out my tongue before breaking a promise I'd made to her, never betrayed the boy's confidence. I dare finally to tell this story, now that so many years have passed since Ariel found rest in his Cuban grave.

It was Anita whom Tere and I felt most sorry for. She truly knew nothing of her brother's illness and impending death. Rita and Natán were careful to buy her a gift every time they came home with something for Ariel. And no young girl in La Habana those days wore clothes as stunning as those that hugged Anita's adorably plump body. Tere loved to iron the pleats in Anita's dresses and skirts, and she has never forgotten how luxurious the fabric felt to her and how soft, softer than freshly plucked rose petals. But Anita was intelligent and perceptive and she noticed that her brother received no scoldings, even when he refused to eat any of his dinner or failed to do his Yiddish homework. And Anita saw that everyone in the Levi family watched over the boy intently. They had eyes only for him. She adored her younger brother, adored him passionately, but she couldn't control the jealous rage that began to overtake her as she felt herself ignored in those last weeks of his life, never knowing that her fury was her good-bye to him. Deprived of understanding, Anita would rush out of the living room when Ariel wanted to play with his train set, or she would bury her head in a book and pay no attention when Ariel crooned a tango song while accompanying himself on the accordion.

Anita one day refused to do her Yiddish homework too. By this time, Tere had taken the two children to enough private classes with their Yiddish tutor, a red-haired schoolteacher by the name of Frida Livak, that she knew many words in Yiddish, by sound, if not by letter. She would sit between Anita and Ariel in the hour before dinnertime and whisper into their ears the Yiddish words they had learned in their lessons. I believe that if it hadn't been for Tere, the children would have turned their backs on the language of their ancestors. They refused to do their Yiddish homework, those two children, in the days when the angel of death took up residence with them, but Tere made sure they did it in spite of themselves. She would send Ariel to his grave prepared to communicate with the Jewish spirits who had not sailed to Cuba and could not speak Spanish. And she would keep Anita from despising her ancestral tongue because of the fit of rage that boiled inside her heart without her knowing why. The girl, through no fault of her own, had lived a life so enchanted she could not fathom that this rage of hers, burning relentlessly, was grief's messenger and that her brother would soon be snatched from her.

Tere spent all her days with the children because Natán and Rita were occupied in their store, Casa Tarzán. Business was booming and they had to oversee their employees, whose hands could wander into the cash register when they thought no one was looking. Natán and Rita were earning more money selling suitcases and handbags in those sad days of 1954 than they had ever earned. It was a bitter blessing and its meaning was not lost upon Natán, whom Tere says used to awaken very early, before the sun came out, and pace back and forth in the kitchen after sipping a strong cup of Cuban coffee that lacked even a sprinkling of sugar. A couple of times she was unable to sleep in the morning and she beheld him mumbling to himself, or, she thought, uttering what seemed like a prayer, asking over and over, "What good is money if I can't save my son? What good is money?" His voice broke, yet he did not weep. He never wept. He was one of those people who came into the world with tearless eyes.

Many years had passed since Máximo Glinienski hurled his curse at Natán Levi on a dark night in Agramonte, but neither had forgotten about it. They did not speak of the curse, at least not during moments when Tere or I could have overheard their conversation. They did not need to speak. The tension that hung in the air between the two men was a storm cloud waiting to explode.

It was both beautiful and cruel that their sons, Pablo and Ariel, only a year apart in age, adored one another and were closer than brothers. The two boys, despite the enmity of their fathers, enjoyed many afternoons together riding their bicycles around the Parque Central. Pablo's bicycle was a flimsier model than Ariel's and had only one speed, probably because it was made in Cuba rather than in England, but the boys didn't pay attention to these petty things. The breeze blew on their faces and they felt free. Ariel's arms and legs were by then so puffy from the illness that he could barely push the pedals of his bicycle. He lost his balance easily. Tere watched him like a hawk to be sure he didn't fall. But he was a child, no one could take that away from him, and he needed to play hard, even at the cost of dropping to bed overcome by fatigue and stiff limbs. Every piece of pavement in the Parque Central registered the tread of these boys as they spun their wheels between the benches.

One afternoon, as if to say good-bye, to the park, to their boyhoods, to each other, Ariel and Pablo asked if they could have their picture taken by a street photographer. Tere and I paid for the picture of the boys, posing beside their bicycles, the statue of José Martí and the royal palms in the background. To this day I conserve that photograph of two white boys suspended tranquilly before the threshold of death. For years this image has been nestled in the same box with the photographs of my own black children.

The last night of his life Ariel got into bed with Tere and slept in her arms until the crack of dawn. She caressed his hair, which ached all the way to the roots on the night he lay dying. Yet his body, Tere says, was weightless. If a spirit could be held in a human embrace, she felt she was holding Ariel's spirit. Half a century later, whenever Tere and I talk about that last night she spent with Ariel, she gets goosebumps on her arms. She says she can't describe what she felt holding the boy, but she remembers thinking he was clinging to life by the roots of his hair, which was why they hurt so badly, but once he let go she knew he would forget the word for pain and death would take him gently.

In the pale morning light Tere led the boy, who was in a state between waking and sleeping, to the bedroom of Natán and Rita. Tere knocked on the door and Natán came to open it. His face was ashen after weeks of sleeplessness and unanswered prayers. From the bedroom, Rita called out, "What is it, Natánsito? Who's there?" Natán always protected his wife from terrible truths. He knew immediately that his son would die that day, but to Rita he called back that everything was fine and that she should keep sleeping until Chela, the cook, had buttered toast and coffee ready for her. He stretched out his arms toward Ariel and seemed to gather him up piece by piece, forcing the boy's body and spirit to cling together a little longer. Then he turned back to Tere and said he would get dressed quickly and he asked her to help the boy slip on street clothes because they needed to get him to the hospital. Tere remembers that she picked out for Ariel a freshly washed and starched white linen shirt and a pair of beige shorts, pleated in the front, for his final journey through the streets of La Habana. She had to dress him like a baby because he kept drifting in and out of consciousness. She still had holy water left from the shrine of San Lázaro and she used it to freshen Ariel's hair. She made sure his hands were clean. And she took a final look at his feet before she covered them with socks and shoes. Tere says that Ariel knew he would not return home. He kissed her and said good-bye. His parting words to her were, "Take care of my sister. Please never leave our family."

She released him to his father and they stepped out of the house into a sudden thunderstorm. Tere ran after them with an umbrella and she remembers seeing Ariel tilting his head back and opening his mouth to taste the rain. At five in the afternoon of that day, which was the twenty-second of October, Ariel died in the arms of his father Natán Levi. It rained as if the world were ending. The last taste of life Ariel took with him was the taste of rain.

His mother, Rita, fainted when she heard the news of her son's death and she fainted again at the funeral. His sister, Anita, was inconsolable and would not forgive her parents for having withheld from her the knowledge that her brother was dying. The funeral, held the next day, was large, and it was attended not only by the entire Levi family and Ariel's teachers and school-mates from the Centro Israelita, but by several hundred *polacos* of the community. The rain cleared and the sun returned, hot and blinding. A long row of cars inched their way from La Habana to the Jewish cemetery in Guanabacoa, a town famous for its *santeros* and *paleros* descended from African slaves. At the cemetery the women wore out their wrists cooling themselves with their Spanish fans, while the men dabbed at their sweaty faces with their monogrammed handkerchiefs. The rabbi spoke words in Hebrew that brought streams of tears to the eyes of Máximo Glinienski, while Natán Levi still could not cry. Even when it came time for Natán Levi to lift the shovel and throw dirt upon the coffin of his son, no tears flowed.

Ariel was buried in his grave. He became, for all eternity, part of the soil of Cuba. He would be of the island, always of the island. He would never leave us. He would never know exile. Death had made him ours. Ours for as long as Olokún, in the ocean depths, remained merciful and let our island keep float-ing above the water.

About the Contributors

Ruth Behar is the author of *Translated Woman: Crossing the Border with Esperanza's Story* (Beacon Press, 1994) and *The Vulnerable Observer: Anthropology that Breaks Your Heart* (Beacon Press, 1997). She is currently at work on an ethnographic novel, *Nightgowns from Cuba,* and a documentary film, *Adio Kerida: A Cuban Sephardic Journey.* She is Professor of Anthropology at the University of Michigan.

Andrew Causey is an artist and anthropologist, and a faculty member at Columbia College, Chicago. Although his perceptions of culture and environment have been nudged and bent by his visual experiments in caricature, surrealism, and expressionism, the story printed here presents a comparatively dry and factual account of an actual experience.

Ron Emoff has been a migrant farmworker, an auto and motorcycle mechanic, an art restorer, an inner-city schoolteacher in Cleveland, a potter, a musician, and a Ph.D. recipient in ethnomusicology (University of Texas at Austin). He is currently Assistant Professor of Ethno/Musicology at Ohio State University–Newark. He has published a book on his research in Madagascar, *Recollecting from the Past: Musical Practice and Spirit Possession on the East Coast of Madagascar* (Music and Culture Series, Wesleyan University Press).

Ben Feinberg's first job was working, at the age of 11, as an intern for the entomologist in charge of exotic insects and such at the Museum of Natural History in New York. Later, he received a Ph.D. in anthropology from the University of Texas at Austin in 1996. He currently teaches at Warren Wilson College in Asheville, North Carolina, and spends some time every year in the Sierra Mazateca of Oaxaca, Mexico.

Katherine J. Hagedorn is Associate Professor of Music at Pomona College in Claremont, California, where she teaches courses on the performance traditions of Latin America and the African diaspora, as well as classes on ethnomusicological theory and method. Professor Hagedorn also directs Pomona's ethnomusicology program, which features a Balinese gamelan gong kebyar, a rotating ensemble-in-residence (Ghanaian drumming, flamenco guitar, Afro-Cuban percussion, etc.), a concert and lecture series, and an interdisciplinary plan of study. Her research, carried out in Cuba and the United States, focuses on Afro-Cuban religious performance and its transformation into folkloric theatre, with an emphasis on the central role of *batá* drumming. Her book based on this research, *Divine Utterances: The Performance of Afro-Cuban Santería,* was published in 2001 by the Smithsonian Institution Press. Trained as a classical pianist, Dr. Hagedorn has performed music from the West African, Afro-Cuban, and Indonesian percussive traditions since the late 1980s. She has a B.A. in Comparative Language and Literature from Tufts University, an M.A. in International Relations from Johns Hopkins University, and an M.A. and Ph.D. in Ethnomusicology from Brown University. Dr. Hagedorn has taught at Pomona College since 1993, and in 2000 was the recipient of the prestigious California Professor of the Year award, sponsored by the Carnegie Foundation for the Advancement of Teaching and the Council for the Advancement and Support of Education.

Karen Tranberg Hansen is Professor of Anthropology at Northwestern University. As an urbanite and world traveler, she specializes in urban anthropology and African studies. Her personal interests in housekeeping, cuisine, and couture are reflected in her books: *Distant*

Companions: Servants and Employers in Zambia 1900–1985 (Cornell University Press, 1989); *African Encounters with Domesticity* (editor; Rutgers University Press, 1992); *Keeping House in Lusaka* (Columbia University Press, 1997); and *Salaula: The World of Secondhand Clothing and Zambia* (University of Chicago Press, 2000). She distrusts authority, as her chapter in this collection demonstrates.

David Henderson has been a Visiting Assistant Professor at Pomona College and the University of Oklahoma and currently teaches in the Music Department at Saint Lawrence University. His first attempt at doing ethnographic work, as a freshman in an expressive culture class, was at Disneyland. Since 1987, he has been doing research on music and social change in the Kathmandu Valley of Nepal.

Laurel Kendall is Curator in Charge of Asian Ethnographic Collections at the American Museum of Natural History. She also teaches in the Anthropology Department at Columbia University. Recognized as a leading anthropologist of Korea, with more than a quarter-century of experience, she has also worked in China, Japan, and Vietnam. She is the author of *Getting Married in Korea: Of Gender, Morality, and Modernity* (University of California Press, 1996); *Shamans, Housewives, and Other Restless Spirits: Women in Korean Ritual Life* (University of Hawaii Press, 1985), and *The Life and Hard Times of a Korean Shaman: Of Tales and the Telling of Tales* (University of Hawaii Press, 1988). With Charles F. Keyes and Helen Hardacre, she was a coeditor and contributor to *Asian Visions of Authority: Religion and the Modern Nation State* (University of Hawaii Press, 1995). She was coproducer with Diana Lee of the video *An Initiation* Kut *for a Korean Shaman,* and has consulted on several other documentary film projects dealing with Korea.

Amitava Kumar is the author of *Passport Photos* (2000) and *Bombay–London–New York* (2002). He is the editor of several collections of essays on teaching, including *World Bank Literature* (forthcoming). Kumar was also the scriptwriter for the prize-winning documentary *Pure Chutney* (1998).

Kirin Narayan's love for stories is woven through her work as an anthropologist, a folklorist, and a writer. She has written two books exploring storytelling in India: *Storytellers, Saints and Scoundrels: Folk Narrative in Hindu Religious Teaching* (which won the 1990 Victor Turner Prize for Ethnographic Writing) and *Mondays on the Dark Night of the Moon: Himalayan Foothill Folktales* (in collaboration with Urmila Devi Sood). She has also written a novel, *Love, Stars and All That.* The chapter in this volume is drawn from her new novel, tentatively titled *Becoming a Foreigner.*